RETIRE IN PRACTICE

RETIRE IN PRACTICE

Living a Lifestyle of Leisure without Sacrificing Your Bottom-line

Dr. Jay Handt and Kathi Handt
with Stephanie Gunning

Foreword by Eric Plasker, D.C.

New York Chiropractic Press
New York, NY

New York Chiropractic Press
NYChiropracticPress.com

For information about special discounts for bulk purposes, please phone 1-845-642-0956 or email orders@NYChiropracticPress.com.

Interior design by Gus Yoo
Cover design by Gus Yoo
Cover Photo by Ryan Handt

978-0-9857216-0-2 (paperback edition)
978-0-9857216-1-9 (digital edition)

1. Personal finance 2. Entrepreneurship 3. Small business 4. Healthy living 5. Success 6. Chiropractic 7. Motivational self-help

To our children, Josh, Ryan, and Morgan

.

CONTENTS

Acknowledgments

We would like to express our gratitude to the many people who have contributed to our lives and the creation of this book.

From Jay: To my father, Arthur, the smartest man I ever met. From the time I was very young, he told me to work for myself. He said: When you work for someone else, your life is theirs. When you work for yourself, your life is yours. And when you work with others, there's no limit to what you can accomplish. The world is yours. He also taught me that if you don't have anything good to say, don't say anything—only put your two cents into a conversation if it's going to change the outcome positively. Your conversations are about getting results, resolving conflict, and making a positive impact on someone's life and on the world. Enough said.

To my mother, Carole, for her favorite line: "You want to do what?!" Which is usually followed by, "Where are you going now?" Both of these questions have inspired me never to stop learning, growing, and experiencing all the world has to offer.

To my sister, Ellen, who has always believed in me and thought I could do anything and be the best at everything.

To my in-laws, Gladys and Julian Martin, who said, "Take my daughter . . . please!" This has been the best advice I ever took.

And, to my wife, Kathi, to whom I owe my entire world: Thank you for always being there in the good times, and for making the bad times good. Thanks for knowing when to push me, and more importantly, when to pull me through. I dedicate this book to you, and more importantly, I dedicate my life to you.

From Kathi: To my dad, Julian, who taught me, from a very early age, that the human spirit pre-dates religion, and all people, regardless of their race, creed, or color, come from the same source. He taught me to be tolerant, loving, and patient with all living creatures.

To my mom, Gladys, who taught me to be strong, stick to my beliefs, and not be swayed by the thinking of others. She always encouraged me to pursue my dreams, no matter what anyone else thought about them.

To my brother, Paul, for always making me laugh, especially when we were kids. His sense of humor and crazy actions can change my state in seconds! He has made me realize that laughter is the best medicine.

To my in-laws, Arthur and Carole, who accepted me with open arms into their family and love me unconditionally.

And to my husband, Jay, who saw the best there was in me, even when I doubted myself, who opened my world and my life to chiropractic, and who has always stood by me so that we can grow together. Thank you for always being there, for loving me more than I thought anyone ever could. I dedicate this book to you, Jay, with all my love.

From both of us: We are grateful to our children, Josh, Ryan, and Morgan, who taught us that you can't be a messiah in your own backyard. For that reason, we have chosen to come to your backyard to play! They taught us about unconditional love and opened our minds to the idea that you can enjoy and experience all the wonders of the world no matter what your age. Through traveling with our kids while they were young, we were always able to see the world through children's eyes: no prejudice, no preconceived ideas...just pure wonder, magic, amazement, and unstoppable curiosity about everything.

To Josh, who taught us that looking at something and seeing something are not the same, and that there is power in the vivid pictures we create in our mind.

To Ryan, who taught us that touching and feeling are completely different, and that there is immense power in human emotions.

To Morgan, who taught us that hearing someone and truly listening to them are totally different and that there are magical powers in the words we use.

And to our daughter-in-law, Meredith, who has brought laughter and an incredible sense of humor to our home, a gift that is so important in our lives!

We would also like to acknowledge the following individuals:

Stephanie Gunning, our editor and co-writer, without whom this book would not exist.

Dr. Chuck Ribley, who opened our eyes to a truly innate way of living and taught us that there is an abundant universe that is always, always, always on our side.

Ruth Ribley, for teaching us that we are always in the right place at the right time, with the right people, for the right reason, to make a positive difference in our lives and in the world.

Dr. Sid Williams, who taught us to give, serve, and love out of a sense of abundance.

Dr. Guy Riekeman, who taught us to dream even bigger.

Dr. Jim Dubel, who taught us that it's okay to be a bull in a china shop when you're changing the world.

Dr. Joe Dispenza, who inspired us to grow our brains by filling our emotional bank account with amazing experiences and never-ending learning.

Dale Lamb, who opened up our world to the magic of NLP and gave us the language to transform lives.

Dr. Kevin Fogarty who taught us the true meaning of friendship.

Dr. Ernie Landi, who taught us the meaning of CANI, constant and never-ending improvement in pursuit of making a difference in people's lives, and to Brenda Landi, for always keeping it light and funny!

Dr. Sharon Gorman, who taught us the power of duplicity and that when you let go of your ego, your vision expands exponentially.

Drs. Jeanne Williamson and John Hilley, who taught us that miracles happen when you keep believing and don't give up.

Dr. Kenneth Harris, to whom we owe our chiropractic direction, principles, and chiropractic life.

FOREWORD

Eric Plasker, D.C.

As I write this foreword for *Retire in Practice*, I do not feel like I am working. I feel retired. Dr. Jay, Kathi, and I have been friends for a long time, so I know they walk their talk, and this is one of the most practical and important books that working professionals can incorporate into their lives.

When I first met Jay and Kathi at New Beginnings Chiropractic Seminars, one of our favorite, mutual *Retire in Practice* gathering places, I noticed several things about them that stood out. First, they were passionate about their work. Second, they seemed always to be having fun, they were successful, they traveled, and they had a beautiful family. They were involved. All of these things are also true today. They are retired in practice!

In 2011, when they decided to become the first 100 Year Lifestyle Affiliate Chiropractic Office in New York City, I was humbled by their commitment and at the same time, super excited to get to know them even better. Jay has become a brainstorming partner with a sharp mind and a purposeful spirit. Kathi continues to grow in her leadership, and all of their kids are engaged in their lives and careers in a manner that is aligned with the principles of this book.

When I researched and wrote the financial chapters of *The 100*

Year Lifestyle, it became clear to me that the traditional concept of retirement was outdated. First, because people are living longer than ever, most people have not saved enough money to support their potential extended life span. Second, it is extremely common that when people retire in the traditional sense, they often become sick with a serious condition. On the other hand, the people who are living long, healthy lives continue to be involved in meaningful work that they are passionate about. I remember interviewing Papa Jack Weil who continued going to the office until the age of 107. When I asked him why, he responded, "What else would I do? I love my work." This is such an important aspect of a fulfilling life that is also filled with abundance.

A very important perspective of this book is that Dr. Jay and Kathi are not financial planners. They are practice owners. They are professionals. It is all too common that professionals get advice from financial people and do not follow it, understand it, or implement it. This often happens because there can be a disconnection in the communication between the professional and the financial expert. Since Dr. Jay and Kathi are professionals who have retired in practice, you will find a simple, realistic connection to their principles.

The concepts in *Retire in Practice* are easy to grasp and implement. They are not overwhelming, so do not procrastinate in getting started. They have been chunked down into a simple plan that, if you follow it, will help you retire in practice, live your best life every day, and enjoy the sensational, abundance-filled life you deserve.

Dr. Eric Plasker,
Bestselling author of *The 100 Year Lifestyle*
100YearLifestyle.com

INTRODUCTION
HOW IT ALL BEGAN

"Motivation is what gets you started. Habit is what keeps you going."
—JIM ROHN

Many years ago, our friend Terry, who is a dentist, invited us to go skiing in Utah. At first we were hesitant to agree because neither of us had ever skied and we were a bit nervous about the cost of going out West from New York: paying for the airfare, the clothing, the equipment, and all of the other expenses that would go along with a high-end ski trip. To set our minds at ease, our friend told us that he and his wife had more than enough ski equipment and clothing. He promised we wouldn't have to buy or rent anything! That made us warm up to the idea. He also mentioned that since we'd be close to Salt Lake City we could always enjoy the sites if we didn't enjoy skiing. When we heard this we really started taking the idea seriously.

At this point the trip was beginning to look like a better prospect, but we still weren't quite convinced we should go due to the high cost of staying at a five-star hotel at a prime ski resort, not to mention covering the expense of food. After all, as parents of three young kids, we'd have five mouths to feed. Jay's practice in New York was doing well, but we were careful about maintaining our budget.

So what convinced us to go? The magic words, "The majority of the trip can be written off as a business expense." This piqued our curiosity.

Terry explained that several times a year he traveled to attend continuing education and business seminars, which afforded him the opportunity to deduct the majority of the expenses associated with these trips from his taxes. As a matter of fact, he informed us that this particular Utah trip would include a health profession seminar every morning, and he pointed out that since Jay was a chiropractor, attending the program would definitely be a deductible expense for us. The skiing and tourism of the area during the days would be a bonus.

Long story short, we did go to Utah that year, bringing the kids along with us for a family vacation. We attended a very interesting health conference at The Cliff Lodge and Spa in Snowbird, learning business skills that served us well. And we learned how to ski, and fell in love with skiing. For many years, we made going to this health conference an annual part of our lives, bringing our children along and making it the ultimate family vacation.

Now for the "aha" moment that changed our lives! It was a radical shift in our thinking.

After attending several of these ski trip/health conferences,

ARE YOU SPENDING YOUR LIFE PREPARING FOR LIFE OR ARE YOU LIVING THE TIME OF YOUR LIFE EVERY DAY, CREATING GREAT MEMORIES FOR THE FUTURE?

we realized that we ourselves could create a professional seminar with topics of interest to us and enjoy all the same benefits we'd been enjoying in Utah no matter where we went. So that is just what we did! We got some professional friends together, put together a program of interest to all of our businesses, and took a trip of our own making. In essence, that first seminar we put on ourselves years ago was our first Retire in Practice program.

From there we went on to discover that similar programs were being held by professional groups across the country and around the world that have something to offer every type of businessperson. We've participated in many of those programs. Kathi started a travel agency to facilitate these programs. That's been a great business for her to run on her own terms.

In the past twenty years or so, we've found this form of educational vacation a great opportunity to travel, see the world, learn new things, meet new people, grow our businesses, and bring us closer to making retiring in practice a reality for us.

We take our leisure seriously! We believe in earning more and working less while offering high-value services to our clients.

Our Promise in this Book

Throughout this book, you will learn all of the steps we had to learn and implement so that we could capture the time we needed for frequent travel and days off for living a lifestyle of leisure without compromising the bottom-line of our businesses or our offerings. Jay is a chiropractor. Kathi is a travel consultant. This book is written for small business owners and every type of professional who runs a client-based business: doctors, lawyers, dentists, life and career coaches, therapists, fitness trainers, accountants, editors, teachers, and more. Even employees in corporations and government can find some pearls of wisdom here on enjoying their lives outside the office to the full by making smart choices about how to manage their time, energy, and money.

Our personal journey to make retiring in practice (RIP) a reality began those many years ago in Utah. In this book we promise to share the secrets of how we've done it with all the others who love what they do, do what they love, and, to paraphrase Mark Twain, make their vocations their vacations. It's not just about ski trips, it's also about the behind-the-scenes planning you do to automate, delegate, and eliminate the elements of your business you don't love to do. The RIP lifestyle is about setting systems in place that liberate you from long hours of working, cash flow shortages, and the fallacious idea, "If you want something done well, you have to do it yourself." It's about having the personal and financial confidence to take charge of your happiness and well-being.

We invite you to expand your field of possibilities in regard to your practice, your profession, and your personal life. Learn the secrets to achieving financial freedom, including how to manage staff and associates so that your business runs with or without you there, create multiple income streams (and not necessarily with network marketing), make your money go farther and last longer, increase patient and customer retention, and become a client magnet, while getting the best vacation deals, flying for free, and *more!*

If that sounds good to you, read on.

CHAPTER 1
TAKE YOUR LIFE BACK

"All our knowledge has its origins in our perceptions."
—LEONARDO DA VINCI

You deserve to have a great life! Our definition of a great life is one where you are healthy in body, mind, and spirit, and able to participate actively, and with fulfillment, in both your career and your leisure activities. By this, we mean taking best advantage of your time. After all, there are a finite number of hours in every day, so you have to decide how you're going to use those hours for maximum enjoyment, enrichment, connection, and prosperity. The aim is to prosper so you may live well and love everything you do.

One of the biggest problems that plague people is that they are living for the future, holding off on experiencing pleasure and meaningful activity today in exchange for the possibility of being happy at a later date. They work long, hard hours and sacrifice the time they could be spending with their families for time on the job. Then, when they are with their families they are worn out and stressed. The pressure gets to them and robs them both of energy and of having the satisfying lifestyle that they dream of leading.

Sacrificing today for tomorrow leads to a second, big problem that's rampant in our culture, which is that if we live for the future rather than today, by the time the future arrives we are filled with regrets. Regretting the past comes from not living well in the present. When you sacrifice the time you could be spending with your children, they grow up—and they might even resent you then for not having been around now. You miss special moments that only happen once in a lifetime, as they hit each developmental milestone in their young lives. Furthermore, when you sacrifice the time you could be spending with your parents, they also grow older. By the time you are available to hang out with them, forge an adult bond, and learn from their wisdom and memories they may have become ill or incapacitated, or even have passed away. Taking time to be with an aging parent is a precious gift for you as much as it is for them.

We hope we don't have to advise you of the many issues that can arise when a spouse or romantic partner feels neglected. Overworking creates distance in relationships. As distance grows, wounds occur and resentments grow. Problems fester and a measure of coolness and distrust emerges that often pushes couples apart. From being each other's greatest supporters, intimate partners can become enemies—or even worse, neutral about one another's presence. They can act like strangers as they're passing in the hallway.

For these reasons and so many others, you simply have got to get used to doing the stuff that you enjoy doing now, today, and not waiting for a later date. Tomorrow is an illusion, a concept that only exists in our minds. We never really know if we are going to have another "tomorrow."

Clean up Your Past

Cleaning up the past is a great starting point for taking your life back. Your present activities plant seeds in the garden of the future in which you're going to live, so what you're doing now is creating the future that you're going to look back on. A garden should be filled with beauty. It should nourish the soul and the body. What past will you look back on? Will it hold family, friendship, success, wealth, pleasure, and health, or will it be filled with your regrets about people never met, places never visited, and adventures never experienced?

If you have any unfinished business, you need to take care of it as soon as possible, because you don't want to continue planting seeds that are unwanted in your life's garden. Make a reasonable plan to tackle debt, resolve disagreements, manage problems, honor promises, and show up where and when you need to show up. Reflect on things that you've been tolerating in your life—even the very small things that bug you, like a leaky faucet in the kitchen—and make a list with a date on it for when you're going to address it. Begin with the easiest item on your list and you'll build confidence and excitement about your ability to get things done. Or begin with the item that seems hardest and take back all the mental energy you expended on worrying about it or complaining about it. You'll feel greater and greater relief as the list of what needs to be cleaned up grows shorter.

Cleaning up the past is like weeding your garden and getting rid of litter that has blown into it. It's like times when a refreshing spring rain washes away the mud and debris from a garden path.

> CHANGE YOUR MIND, CHANGE YOUR LIFE. THIS IS ONLY POSSIBLE WHEN YOU CHANGE YOUR ACTIONS. IT'S TAKING ACTION ON YOUR CHOICES.

Now, the trick is to keep your garden clean and only plant in it that which you love or that which will nurture the future you want. Be deliberate.

Seek Balance and Moderation

Foremost in having a good life is having good health. You want to live a healthy life so that you can enjoy it. It is therefore essential to schedule regular personal time to maintain your well-being. This principle is the bottom line reason for retiring while still maintaining your practice. Often when we teach this to people with a heavy workload, they think we're nuts. They tell us, "Boy, if I want to be healthy I'll have to give up eating great tasting food and spend half my life in the gym!" They think, "That's impossible and doesn't sound like fun!"

In reality, you can do bite-sized chunks of everything in moderation and enjoy a healthy life. There is a difference between being healthy and being fit. Neither of us is an extremist by any means or measure. We go through phases in which we exercise more or less, work more or less, and eat more or less. In the end, your goal should be to become balanced in your habits. A compulsion or an addiction to doing either "good things" or "bad things" is not healthy, and we're not advocating it. Aim for a healthy balance and start adding things that are good for your life to your life. You'll find that the more good stuff you add into your life, the less time and energy you'll have to spend on bad stuff.

A healthy lifestyle includes plenty of time for rest and leisure, for exercise, and for joy. Even if you don't yet believe that you are financially ready to work fewer hours in your practice, you

> YOU MUST CARE FOR YOURSELF FIRST IN ORDER TO CARE FOR OTHERS.

need to embrace the philosophy of a balanced lifestyle. It's the most appropriate place to begin making a transition to a better lifestyle. Why? Because your life is like a bicycle wheel. The hub of the wheel is your well-being and each spoke in the wheel is a different facet of your life. When the spokes of a bicycle wheel are evenly tightened and well-balanced with one another, the wheel runs smoothly around its axel. By contrast, if you tighten one spoke more than the others, the wheel doesn't turn smoothly. The same is true for your life. Spending too much in one area of your life will always throw the rest of your life out of balance. Balance gives you a smoother ride.

How many people set goals for their businesses and leave out family and spirituality? When you take time to tighten all the spokes in the wheel of your life and well-being, you'll discover that the moneymaking aspect of your life actually runs smoother.

Get in Tune

We have learned firsthand through running a successful chiropractic practice that if your primary aim is to serve people well, and you view generating profits as secondary, the money shows up. Seriously, the more we give, the wealthier we become and the more personally enriched and rewarded we feel by knowing that we have been of service. If you believe in an abundant universe, then you already know that you only need to find a way to get in tune with the universe. There is a constant flow of energy and abundance among people in this world, including the circulation of money from your clients to you, and you to people who provide you with the goods and services you need and want. Money follows value.

Become a trend spotter. Being successful in business means figuring out what people need, and then figuring out how to give it to them in the way they *want* it. People hate to do and pay for what they need. But they will do just about anything to get and pay for what they *want*. If you look at Jay's business, The New York Chiropractic Life Center, you will see a very different and unique chiropractic office. When you ask the patients about their care, the overall consensus is that they love coming in, having coffee and cookies, and talking with the friendly staff in our waiting room, and they love their chiropractors.

Everyone is greeted with open arms at New York Chiropractic Life Center. They are more excited about the experience than the results. It is an open and friendly environment. Some people even come back to the office following their regular visit just to be part of the energy, have a cup of coffee, and feel appreciated. The secret that Jay knows is that all of his practice members need lifetime care to ensure a long and healthy life...Not an easy sell in a medically oriented society where it's a commonly held belief that you should only take care of yourself when you are sick.

What we do in our office is give practice members what they want: a loving relationship built on trust, gratitude, and appreciation for their being part of our family, having someone who will always listen to them, sharing in their good times and helping them through difficult times, while always striving to exceed their expectations, **and** while giving them what they need packaged in the way they want it. As a result, our office sees generations of practice members, from newborns to super seniors, giving all of them the opportunity to express life fully. Maintaining flow in this practice has come from building positive, long-term relationships.

"If A is a success in life, then A equals X plus Y plus Z. Work is X, Y is play, and Z is keeping your mouth shut!"
—ALBERT EINSTEIN

In the beginning of building any type of business or practice, from a health care practice to an accounting practice, a copyediting business, or a home organizing service, you have to find and attract people. Then you must build strong relationships with them. This comes from giving value and being genuinely concerned that the patients'/ clients'/customers' needs are being met while their expectations are being exceeded. Ten percent of Jay's practice still comes from the first five years he was in business over thirty years ago. Although the Center has moved once, he's worked in the same neighborhood throughout his career. Six people who attended his thirtieth-anniversary party were his patients when he was working in an outpatient clinic as a student at the New York Chiropractic College, which was located in Manhattan at that time.

Once you create trust in your relationships with those who want and also need your services, you can avoid the trap of overworking with its accompanying stress-induced diseases, compensatory behavior and addictions, frustration, resentment, poor family life, and shaky relationships. You can avoid burnout once you understand this idea. That's why you are never too young to retire in practice, and why you are never too old to practice in retirement.

Manage Your Energy, Not Your Time

Time is an illusion. The greatest way to check the veracity of this statement is if you're waiting on line somewhere. Watch how time flows during ten minutes at the post office. Compare this to when you are doing something else you really enjoy, like watching a movie. Hours can disappear in an instant. Think back on the day of your wedding. Time is a subjective experience created to keep us in control of our lives, but it doesn't exist no matter how objectively we try to measure it.

We tend to agree with the underlying theme of Samuel Butler's novel *Erewhon* (1872). In the land called *Erewhon* (which is almost *nowhere*, spelled backwards) clocks are banned. Time was designed to help humanity, but it ended up enslaving people. The hands on the clock began to control and regulate every minute of every day of their lives, replacing their innate creativity and enjoyment of life with rigid scheduling that imprisoned them. In an effort to give people their lives back, clocks were banned, schedules were eliminated, and freedom was restored.

Time is very subjective. So much so that you can literally create the time you need by how you manage it. Stop and think of someone who has accomplished a lot, like Bill Gates from Microsoft or Richard Branson from Virgin Atlantic. Then think of someone who never finishes projects or accomplishes much. We all have the same twenty-four hours! The difference between these two types of people is how they invest their time. Clearly accomplishment is about directing your energy to be efficient and effective in the space allotted to you.

Projects and activities are like gas. Gas will fill whatever space it occupies, big or small. Projects and activities will fill whatever time allotment you provide for it: minutes, hours, days, or weeks! Molecules of gas become diffused and fill up the available space. The same thing happens with time and activity. Most people use the full amount of time they are given for a job or project no matter how much or little time is allotted. Time expands or contracts according to the person who contains it.

To be able to retire in practice, you have to change the way you invest your time. You have to be able to package your projects to create more free time in your life. We've got some ideas about how you can manage time effec-

> *"I must govern the clock, not be governed by it."*
> —GOLDA MEIR

tively, which we'll share with you.

Maximize Your Hourly Effort

Study the biological rhythms in your body. Understanding when you are most productive and least productive is going to make your life easier. Accomplishing tasks in shorter spans of time depends on knowing how your energy cycles every day. Rarely can anyone function longer than ninety minutes at a clip, no matter how their energy cycles naturally. Therefore, to try to do more without taking a break is going to be depleting.

Just knowing this one fact is sufficient to begin planning an effective day.

The average attention span is twenty to twenty-six minutes, and appears to be growing shorter with every new generation! This means you can have three productive periods of attention during one ninety-minute energy cycle. When our kids were in school we taught them how to study by stopping every twenty minutes, putting their books down, standing up and stretching, or drinking a glass of water, then sitting back down and getting back to studying. You can do the same thing when you're working. Every time you take a short break your body clock resets itself.

Your body has innate rhythms that you should take advantage of. Doing so is part of knowing how to utilize your time most effectively. After ninety minutes of doing the same kind of activity (phone calls, seeing patients, bookkeeping, emails, reading, and so on), you also can get a new surge of energy by switching to a different kind of activity. At the very least you need to take a break for a minimum of five minutes (though fifteen minutes is preferable) to rest.

If you've been sitting indoors, take a short, brisk walk outdoors and get some fresh air. Move your limbs and circulate your blood through your muscles and brain. Recent university studies, as reported by the BBC, prove that "people who walk at least five miles a week have bigger brains, better memories, and improved mental ability compared to those who are more sedentary." In fifteen minutes of brisk walking, most people can go a mile.

Reclaim Your Entire Day

You don't have to wait to make a New Year's resolution to begin reclaiming your time. Start today. This said, on whatever day you start we want you to plan forward for one full year. Get yourself a year-at-a-glance calendar. Placing a full year calendar up where you can always see it tends to keep it in the forefront of your mind and makes your actions to follow through on the commitment more concrete! You can use your smart phone as a backup and reminder.

Going forward from the first week, every six to eight weeks circle a weekend. This will be a weekend when you do zero work. It's a real weekend off to rest, regenerate, revitalize, and have fun.

Then, do your best to figure out how you might add a day or two on either side of the weekends you circled—or an extra day on both sides. Those are days you will be giving to yourself in the coming year (your investment, so to speak, in your RIP account).

Most people are familiar with the concept of tithing, where you donate 10 percent of your earnings to a worthy cause. In his classic 1926 book, *The Richest Man in Babylon*, George S. Clason explains that to become wealthy you have to pay yourself first. A parable set in biblical antiquity, it's about two ordinary men who decide to study the success habits of, and you guessed it, the wealthiest man in Babylon. The book expresses what has become our golden rule: You need to pay yourself 10 percent of everything you earn and use the remaining 90 percent for paying bills and all other expenses. That 10 percent, invested over time, guarantees wealth. We all know that at the end of the month when we pay all our bills, more often than not, there is nothing left for us! That is why it is so important to put yourself first, at the top of the list. Pay yourself first and you will find you have enough money for both.

Now, take this concept and apply it to your time. If you take 10 percent of your time for you, and leave 90 percent for everyone and everything else, you can be guaranteed a more meaningful life. If you don't take your time, there will always be someone or something that will. We are advocating that you tithe time to yourself simply because you deserve it. Pay yourself in time off first before you pay others with time "on."

Ten percent of your year is 36.5 days. That's the minimum amount of days we want you to go ahead and put your circled weekends around.

Your goal is to be able to take off all 36.5 days eventually, beginning as soon as possible. If you can't do this yet, the way to maximize the effects of your RIP investment for the time being is to add two vacation days to a weekend. And to really maximize your time investment, tack it on to a holiday weekend giving you a bonus day.

The average employees receive two weeks of paid vacation per year. Using this scenario they can have five long weekends (four or five days apiece) and one full week of vacation during the year.

Of Americans age sixty-five to sixty-nine, 33.6 percent are still working. Of persons over age seventy, 13.5 percent are still working (statistics as of 2005). By 2014, the number of people working into their seventies is expected to grow to 74 percent.

People in our society typically plan a two-week vacation once a year. That's only ten days off. So obviously thirty-six days is more—and more time off is better. But there's another reason to take small amounts of time off, rather than two weeks in a row. Resting for two weeks puts you so far out of your routine that it takes a longer time to get back into the flow when you go back to work. Football has a pre-season of six weeks, because it takes that long to get back in shape. Baseball spring training serves the same purpose. In a business, obviously it's preferable to be fully productive without needing to ramp up.

Taking more frequent, but shorter breaks from your business helps you rest, reenergize, rejuvenate, and refocus without losing momentum. This way you don't need to retrain yourself. Everything comes back to the idea of maximizing your work time so that you accomplish more, quicker.

With a Friday and Monday off, you create a four-day weekend, which gives you plenty of time to travel, play, see family and friends, and sleep to your heart's content. So give this to yourself. And give it to your staff, too, so they also function at their best. As employers, we're happier when the staff doesn't take long times off. Giving everyone mini-vacations is a way to maximize coverage in the office and keep the energy high. What's good for you is also good for your team members. That's a secret of morale and loyalty.

Once you start getting into the flow of taking long weekends every six to eight weeks, then you will find that you can take as much time off at once as you want—perhaps two, or even three, weeks in a row—because you will have trained yourself how to be away. By this we mean that you will be able to put your mind on your business when you're not at work, rather than having your business on your mind. Often we enjoy planning projects and new ventures when we're relaxing on a trip. We literally find it fun. Remember though, extended vacations should not be used as compensation for giving up scheduled mini-vacations. Once they are scheduled in the calendar adhere to long weekends.

Staycations

Another way to give yourself a break is to change something about your environment and your routine without leaving town. Brain growth is essential to being successful and having resilience, and it comes from having novel and surprising experiences. You also need to get away from facing the same stresses. So take a staycation. This is where you stay home on a vacation. Take an afternoon off and go visit a friend. Go visit a relative.

Conversations and connection both can stimulate new ideas.

When the weather is nice we like to go up once a month to visit friends at their house. There we sit out on the deck in the sunshine and talk about the books we've read and the people we've met. We trade ideas and insights, and we laugh together. The purpose of staycationing is to change your environment, change the way you think, change the way you act, and create new belief systems.

New experiences and learning are two ways your brain continues to grow in adulthood. If you're not experiencing something new, then your brain is not growing. And when your brain is not growing it is dying. Joe Dispenza, D.C., wrote a great book on growing the brain, *Evolve Your Brain* (Health Communications Inc., 2007), in which he points out that there are only two ways your brain grows: either by experiencing or by learning something totally new. The caveats are: first, use it or lose it; second, the more you use it, the longer it stays. By doing new things consistently you create new networks of brain cells. Once you establish these brain patterns they become routine and the norm for you.

You can use these rules to get rid of old habits and patterns, too. If you block them, those neural pathways die out. You can substitute a new pathway for an old one in a relatively short amount of time—between thirty and ninety days—if you are consistent.

Handling Fatigue

Brain research shows that working intensely without taking breaks reduces focus and concentration. So do not forget the "twenty-minute rule," especially if you're already feeling fatigued. Your rule of thumb is to do twenty minutes of work followed by a one-minute break. Stand up and move your body. And if your eyes feel fatigued, step away from your computer screen. Look out the window and stare at the horizon. As you shift your focus from a near-focus to a far-focus, you literally give the eye muscles a rest.

When your energy is high, take on your most challenging tasks and get them accomplished. But when you're feeling tired do mundane tasks instead. Employing this simple tactic means that you still can be productive on days when you're not at your best, or during the hours of the day when you're a little bit sluggish. Then you won't waste or lose hours on ineffective effort. File paperwork, straighten up your desk, or do something equally necessary that can be accomplished with low concentration.

Many of the most progressive companies understand that younger generations of workers need stimulation if you want to keep them focused. The baby boomer generation could plod along and be left-handed bolt turners on an assembly line for ten years and be happy. With younger generations that is no longer the case. Recognizing that modern brains are being hardwired by the Internet, smart phones, and television for speed, short bursts of attention, and instantaneous shift in focus, these companies know they have to do more to motivate their workers to enjoy their jobs.

Zappo's is an innovative company that does this well. They offer their workers food breaks and dance breaks (disco music suddenly comes on a loud speaker, for instance), spontaneous volleyball games, and even departmental parades. These offerings keep people from getting burned out and tired. The stimulation resets their energy and actually spikes their creativity. The Huffington Post has a nap room with beds for its employees. People are encouraged to lie down and shut their eyes whenever they feel sleepy.

Flexibility

Think about setting up flexible scheduling in your practice. Have staff people come in during the hours when they are at their best, even those hours are not the typical nine-to-five hours. Maybe one person is a night owl and can handle a later shift. Maybe one is an early bird. If you have clients that want early or late service, match those individuals to the times they are needed—such as evening hours of service or early hours of service.

In some businesses, it might also be appropriate for you or your employees to telecommute two days a week. Telecommuting means handling business remotely, by phone and Internet. This works well for coaches and therapists, and businesspeople who need peace and quiet to get reading and writing done. Cutting down on travel saves time and increases the flexibility of when work takes place, thus giving telecommuters an opportunity to take extra rejuvenation breaks during their work activities or program their work schedule around other priorities in their lives.

How Much Time Do You Pay Yourself?

If you don't take advantage of your time somebody else will. It could be a family member, a colleague or coworker, or a friend. There is always someone who can think of something good to tell you to do with your time or who wants you to give him or her some of your time. If you're someone who has trouble saying no or who has many legitimate obligations to fulfill, you can get ahead of requests by working with your calendar. Blocking things out on paper is a way of seeing in black and white where you can, and even *must*, say no to new requests. After all, there are only twenty-four hours in a day.

As you begin advancing your new priorities, an eye-opening exercise to do for a week is to monitor your time expenditures and get clear about where your time is going. Then reduce waste. Eliminating meaningless, insignificant activity from your daily schedule is like paying yourself a bonus. With the time you reclaim, you can do something you love or do something meaningful for your business. It's a dividend of prioritizing.

Reflection Questions

Ask and answer the following questions.

- What are the five primary areas in your life that you want to balance and bring into harmony with each other?
- Where do you currently need to establish balance?
- What is the first step you need to take in order to restore balance in your life?
- What could you focus your actions on that would make the greatest impact with the least amount of time and energy?
- What stands in the way of you having more time off? How can you change that?
- When was the last time you took time off during which you

didn't call the office to find out what was going on in your absence?

- How many unused sick days, personal days, and vacation days have you accumulated in the past that you could draw upon now or that you've lost forever?
- What was the best vacation you ever took and what about it made it the best?
- What has worked well for you in structuring your days, and how could you repeat and improve on that now and in the future?

Remember what we said at the beginning of the chapter: Your goal now is to design a lifestyle that brings you maximum enjoyment, enrichment, and connection, as well as prosperity. Once you become aware of how you are expending your time and energy, you can begin to align your daily activities with the fulfillment of your true needs and priorities. Committing to frequent rest periods for growth, stimulation, relaxation, and decompression is a tremendous step toward retiring in practice. The next is to organize your finances to support your new lifestyle, which is exactly what we'll take a look at doing in chapter 2, "Manage Your Money."

CHAPTER 2
MANAGE YOUR MONEY

"So many fail because they don't get started—they don't go. They don't over-come inertia. They don't begin."
—W. CLEMENT STONE

Congratulations! You've already taken an important step in the right direction. You made a commitment to play as much as you work, and you took your life back by setting up a new energy-management system on your calendar. Future days off are circled or blocked out, and so your retirement in practice has begun. Give yourself a pat on the back. So now where is the money going to come from to create and sustain your RIP lifestyle? The next step is setting up a comparable money-management system so that your new lifestyle becomes sustainable and even profitable.

If you're like many people we talk to, even though you're open to, and enthusiastic about the idea of retiring in practice your main concern is how to afford it. You might even be thinking, "I can't take that much time off. I just don't have enough money." Even so, we encourage you to stick with the schedule. Personal time is a priority and you deserve to use yours as you see fit. Perhaps the biggest hurdle you need to leap over right now is the very idea that you don't have enough savings or income to take this approach to doing business. There is a way, and we're going to explain it. We're going show you how to set up your financial accounts so that you can move gradually in the direction of enjoying more and more play time. Did you ever see the old Looney Tunes cartoon version of the Aesop's fable "The Tortoise and the Hare"? You know the story: The tortoise and the hare are running a footrace. As the slow-moving tortoise diligently plods his way toward the finish line, the speedy hare runs circles around him and has a ton of fun. Sure, the hare is too confident and loses the race, but he has a great time running it. He knows how to enjoy the beauty of the trip. We want you to have that experience, too. You absolutely deserve to enjoy your life.

Consider this question: Are you playing in life to win or to finish? It's not the same. What if you could be like the hare and get ahead while you're at work, and then, during your play time, slow down and be like the tortoise? You'd still reach the finish line.

The only finish line that matters is financial freedom.

What Is Financial Freedom?

Financial freedom means being able to afford to do what you want to do when you want to do it, with whom you want to do it, without worrying where the money is going to come from. That's the goal. Let's say you wanted to take a $10,000 vacation in Hawaii so you could swim with the dolphins. Let's also say that you wouldn't be able to afford to, today. Does this mean you should forego a vacation altogether? No. You do not have to sacrifice leisure; you just have to find the way that's within your current means. You may have to defer the Hawaiian vacation for a while, but if you plan appropriately for it over time and take the right action steps to follow through on this plan, in the future you'll have the money to cover it. Life is full of choices and opportunities.

Achieving financial freedom is a lot like solving a jigsaw puzzle. You want to put together enough pieces to enable you to live a life that looks like the big picture of what you want. There are many pieces, yet all pieces in the puzzle fall into two main categories:

Active income: income from working, including salaries, wages, and tips.

Passive income: income that you don't have to work for, such as interest from a certificate of deposit or a savings account, stock dividends, returns on investments of some kind, network marketing, or any other stream of passively-generated income. Another term you may have heard for passive income is *residual income*.

Once your passive income exceeds your expenses by one dollar you've achieved financial freedom. At that moment, you go from "having to work" to "choosing to work." It gives you a whole new level of liberation. And when you set up your finances so that the passive income you make *exceeds* your expenses, and you continue earning income by doing something you are passionate about, the spread between your passive income and expenses becomes progressively larger, which in turn creates an even more astonishing level of freedom. And there's a bonus, once you no longer have to work. You can work simply because you enjoy it. Then you can do whatever you love doing most.

The key to making the financial freedom process work for you is your knowledge of what your expenses are. Most people think they need much more money than they actually do in order to reach financial independence.

At one of our financial independence programs in Snowbird, Utah, given about twenty years ago, we started the session by asking, "How much money do you need to be financially free?" We had participants take turns sharing their answers. One woman left a lasting impression of how great the gap can be between what someone thinks they need and what they actually need!

The woman, who was a massage therapist, told the group that she needed three million dollars in the bank to be financially free. We decided to use her as our group example and worked through our discovery process.

First, we asked for her current yearly income, which was $35,000. We asked if her income met all her expenses, to which she replied yes. Then we asked if she had any outstanding debt (mortgage, auto loans, credit cards, and so on). She didn't. So in applying the concept of passive income, what she needed was to have enough money in investments to generate a minimum of $35,000 in interest and dividends. And in actuality, her expenses were lower than $35,000. We learned that if she stopped working, her expenses would drop 25 percent, so she really needed only about $26,500 in passive income at most.

Now, the big question was this: How much would she need to invest in order to generate that amount of interest per year? At the time of the program, interest rates were higher than they are now; meaning, she could receive a 10-percent return on her investments. In reality, she didn't need three million dollars. In fact, she only needed $265,000 in the bank! If she continued to work and keep the same expenses, she would need $350,000 to retire. At those amounts, it became much more attainable, and that possibility motivated her to work a little more and design a savings plan to reach her goal as soon as possible, all without compromising her time freedom.

ARE YOU CREATING MEMORIES OR REGRETS? ON THEIR DEATHBEDS, PEOPLE RARELY REGRET THE THINGS THAT THEY DID. THEY REGRET THE THINGS THEY DIDN'T DO.

Today, she actually lives the RIP lifestyle!

Clarity Is Powerful

Having a clear picture of your current financial situation is essential. You need to know where you are before you can decide what action steps you need to take to get where you want to be. Some people use accounting software to manage their bookkeeping, other people just use a checkbook register. Either way is fine. But you need to get down on paper the current facts about your money. If you're not already tracking it regularly, begin monitoring the flow on a monthly basis (some people also track daily).

Here are the four aspects of your financial picture you need to look at:

- *Monthly income*: How much is coming in? Where does it come from?
- *Savings*: How much do you have in savings? How much do you save on a regular basis?
- *Monthly expenses*: How much is going out? Where is it going?
- *Debt*: How much do you owe? To whom do you owe it? (It's good also to know the minimum amount that has to be paid down each month.) And what is the percentage of interest you are paying on each debt?

If you find that your monthly expenses are greater than your income, there are only two healthy ways to resolve the problem: either cut your expenses or raise your income—or even better, do both. Taking on additional debt by using credit cards or getting a loan from the bank (or a family member or friend) is going to take you further away from your goal of financial freedom. So that's not a healthy way to manage your finances on a regular basis.

Let's talk for a moment about credit cards. They are like the devil's spawn. Pure evil. If you pay the minimum balance on credit cards at the rates banks are charging at present, you'll only be paying off your interest and never making a dent in the principle that you charged. This is how people often get stuck in debt. Ideally, if you use a credit card to pay for a purchase you will need to pay it off in full by the end of the month. If you're in the habit of carrying balances on your cards, now is the time to break this habit.

Likewise, you do not want to get behind on your taxes. The IRS is the scariest kind of creditor there is, because they have so much power. Think of movie star Wesley Snipes, who failed to pay $1 million dollars in taxes after earning $38 million dollars over a ten-year period, and then ended up serving a three-year prison term. It's clear a guy like him just needed to plan better. People who work for companies that do IRS reporting have money taken out of their paychecks on a regular basis that goes toward taxes. But if you're an independent contractor, you have to practice setting aside enough money to pay your estimated taxes on time. Otherwise you're going to get slammed with a big payment to make come April.

If you know the future dates on which certain quarterly, annual, or other occasional expenses, like taxes and balloon payments on a mortgage, are due, it's a very good idea to list those key dates and amounts on paper. The better you anticipate future needs for money, as well as the timing with which the money must flow out of your hands, the easier it is to be prepared to meet those needs. Clarity is a powerful financial tool.

When you have added up your monthly income (including paychecks, savings interest, stock dividends, and other investment income) and have added up your monthly expenses (including, but not limited to credit card payments, loan payments, rent, mortgage, utilities, and all other living expenses, as well as any money that you have put into any type of savings), compare the income and expense totals. If your monthly expenses are greater than your income, it means you have lost control of the flow of your money.

In other words: income + credit charges = expenses + savings.

Assuming that you have a balanced income/expense sheet, and know the total amount of your debt and your savings, you now have a clear picture of where you are financially.

Streams of Income

To put yourself squarely on the path to financial freedom that we're advocating—one where you are playing at least as much as, if not more than you are working—you need to focus on generating passive income and active income simultaneously. Remember, the minute you make a dollar more in passive income than you spend, you're on this path.

So go back and figure out where your income comes from in different categories you assign according to your own business activities. Perhaps money is coming in from a salary, doing consultations or therapy, network marketing commissions, sales of products (books, audios, videos, vitamin supplements, or other merchandise), referral or affiliate fees, speaker's fees, interest, dividends, and the fees you receive for teaching courses or leading workshops, and don't forget interest and dividends from your investment savings. It can be illuminating to discover which specific areas of your business are generating the most income for you with the least effort. These may not be the same areas you thought they'd be.

Once you have a list of income streams, shift your time, energy, and attention from pursuing high effort-low reward activities to

> *"Change is simple. Thinking about change is difficult."*
> —ERIC PLASKER, D.C.

low effort-high reward activities. Also consider adding additional passive income streams into the mixture. We'll talk about a variety of opportunities you could create for yourself in a later chapter.

Furthermore, if you are not involved in network marketing or generating other forms of passive income on a regular basis, you absolutely have to begin to gather some savings together. Without passive income or savings, you won't have sufficient money to spend during your scheduled periods of leisure.

Setting Up Your Financial Accounts

Jay's father was a responsible money manager. As a kid growing up, he watched his father's behavior carefully. His father developed an envelope savings account system for his planned expenses. And he paid cash for everything. He had a different envelope for whatever he wanted. If he knew he'd need to buy a new car in three years, he made an envelope for the car and labeled it "car." If he wanted a stereo, he created an envelope for it labeled "stereo." The same was true for healthcare, photography, and travel. Every time he got a paycheck, he would divide the money, putting a percentage into every envelope. Whatever money was left over after contributing to the envelopes, he used for living expenses. If he didn't have much money left on a given month after divvying it up to meet his anticipated needs, then he would cut back on living expenses. His family would eat pasta that month instead of steak.

You can do the same thing with bank accounts that Jay's father did with envelopes. Banks don't mind; they'll gladly let you have as many accounts with them as you want. We recommend making a firm commitment to divide every paycheck you receive by specific percentages that are deposited into your different accounts. At first, this might seem strange and possibly difficult to accomplish. Some people notice that they have to tighten their belts initially in certain areas of their expenditure. There's a gap between the amount they want to sock away and what's coming in. After three months, however, they don't feel any sense of scarcity. It's remarkable, but the universe will find ways to fill in the gaps in your income streams—so long as your intentions are well defined.

We recommend that you do the following. Set up the following bank accounts.

- *Financial freedom account.* Pay yourself first. Before you pay taxes, rent, bills, or anything else for that matter, from now on, just as soon as you receive income, a predetermined percentage of it goes right into this account. If you can, we recommend that you set aside 10 percent. That way, in the same way you are now tithing 10 percent of your time to yourself, you'll be tithing money to yourself. And, if that percentage is not yet manageable, start lower. You can always go up the scale later. The important thing is to make a commitment to pay yourself first. This should be your number one commitment.

- *Tax account (federal, state, and local).* You don't want to be surprised when it's time to pay the taxes. Tax rates are graduated for different levels of income, and the rates are a matter of public record. Here you need to set aside a percentage that matches your own tax rate. You may need to do a little research to figure that out, or put in a phone call to your accountant. Whatever the rate turns out to be—and typically this rate lies in the range between 20 and 38 percent—the percentage you put into this account is non-negotiable. We actually put in an additional percentage point or two as a buffer. The worst thing that will happen is that you have money left over that you can move into other accounts. It needs to be separated from the rest of your money before you divvy up money for any additional expenses.

Now, if you are having trouble meeting your taxes, or you owe back taxes, you should know that the IRS is usually willing to set up a payment plan, and sometimes even to compromise on outstanding taxes. They'd rather get something from you than nothing by forcing you into declaring bankruptcy. If you and the IRS agree upon a payment schedule for back taxes you owe, you'll need to set up another account to handle them. Your tax account is for future taxes.

- *Fun account.* Most savers resent saving. They are so persistently working to pay their bills and become debt free that they don't have anything to show for themselves at the end of the day. Basically, they are working for everyone else and life sucks. It's similar to our son Josh's friend, who became a lawyer. Although earning upwards of $90,000 a year, he was working ninety hours a week for his firm. Because there was so little personal time, he soon got bitter and resentful. Perpetually deferring gratification with money also makes people bitter and resentful. It doesn't take long to feel mad and bad, so you need to reward yourself with a fun account.

  Your Fun account has a couple of imperatives attached to it: First, every three months, the account must be emptied. Second, you are not allowed to spend your fun money on anything you need. Imagine this money fell out of heaven, so it is purely designed to give you a good time and bring you pleasure. At the end of three months, the account might only hold enough for dinner and a movie, but you must spend it on that, rather than on something you need, like groceries. Instead of car repairs, spend it on a night in a hotel.

  Use this money to have fun on the days off that you

planned in your calendar. The percentage you put into the account is your choice, however you might consider starting with 3 to 5 percent. Since, on average, personal income grows over the years, the amount of fun money at your disposal is likely to grow.

- *Debt reduction account.* Having added up your total debt, and also determined the minimum monthly payments that are due to creditors (for credit charges, bank loans, tuition loans, personal loans, mortgages, and so on), you need to set aside sufficient income to cover the minimum and a bit more. Use the funds in this account that exceed your minimum monthly payments due to pay down your various debts one by one, starting with whichever has the highest interest rate.

The way to get ahead on debt is that after one interest-bearing debt has been paid off, add the amount you would have applied to it to the amount you are using to pay off the next-highest interest rate debt. Then do the same with the next debt and the next after that, until all of your debts are all gone. When you are debt free, divide the percentage you were paying into this account in half, and add those percentage points to your Financial Freedom account and your Fun account.

- *Bailout account.* Another account you need is a Bailout account. This is an emergency savings account to be used for unforeseen expenses (for instance, major auto repairs, home repairs, dental and health crisis expenses, job, or income loss). Keep contributing a percentage into this account until you accumulate enough money to cover six months of living expenses. You don't have to keep feeding money into it once you reach this goal level. It doesn't require any more funds to be added unless your expenses increase. This money is your security blanket. Especially if you are a sole proprietor, you need to reserve six months for your rent and food. This money is for any kind of life emergencies you face.

- *Living expense account.* This final account is the one that should be linked to your checkbook. Its purpose is to handle the payment of routine expenses, including fixed expenses, like rent, water, electricity, insurance, phone, Internet, and gas; and soft expenses, like groceries, chewing gum, clothing, movies, and so forth. Whatever money is left over after you pay your allotted percentages into the other accounts should be deposited here. You certainly do not have to use up the funds in this account every month. Nonetheless, the balance will tend to go up and down more rapidly than the balance in your other accounts. This may be the area where cutbacks are necessary if you have a shortfall in income.

Setting Your Percentages

You choose the percentages for each account. No one else can tell you that 25 percent or 10 percent is the right amount for a specific purpose in your life. You have to sit and think about it carefully and then make your decision. As you set the percentages, we suggest that you use the rule of thumb that you can raise, but never lower the percentage points (the only exceptions are your Bailout and Debt Reduction accounts, for reasons stated above).

When you're initially figuring out how much is needed for your living expenses, which is one of the main determinants in setting percentages, it's a good practice to keep a log for two weeks of everything you buy. Money often leaves our pockets in little drips and drabs. By cutting back on stupid, little items and impulse purchases, and by making educated choices and reprioritizing your expenses, you may find your expenses going down. A woman attending one of our programs said that she didn't have any extra money. Through some simple questioning, we found out that she was going to Starbucks for coffee seven days a week, and sometimes twice a day. When she looked at her log she figured out that she was going to save close to $2,000 dollars a year just by not going there and making her own coffee. Of her own free will, she decided that investing in her Fun account was more important to her.

Ever since then, one of the first questions we ask people who attend our Retire in Practice workshops is: "Do you go to Starbucks?" The majority of people will answer yes. Then we ask: "How often do you go to Starbucks during the week?" Many respond, "Five days a week." "And what's your favorite drink to order? And how much does it cost?" we continue. "Such and such, at five bucks a pop," they reply. Everyone laughs then because we all know they are pissing away their money—literally.

The easiest time to start putting a percentage of your income into different accounts is actually when you're not making much money. If you are only making $100 a week, it's easy to put away ten dollars. You still have $90 dollars for expenses. When you go from $100 to $150 a week you're putting away $15 and you have $5 dollars more in your pocket. That seems like almost the same amount. But once you're earning $10,000 a week, it seems harder to put away $1,000. Of course, it is only difficult between your ears. For now you've got $9,000 for living expenses. But typically people raise their expenses as their income goes up. It would be easy to save that money if they would merely keep

> THOUGHTS WITHOUT ACTION ARE LIKE MENTAL MASTURBATION. THEY FEEL GOOD, BUT DON'T CREATE ANYTHING!

their expenses down. That $1,000 wouldn't seem difficult to save and they'd be closer to their ultimate goal of financial freedom.

Young people especially are likely to raise their expenses whenever they get more money. They go from a one-bedroom apartment to a two-bedroom apartment, and in doing so keep running in place. Expenses tend to expand, and this is a common trap.

Most people don't realize that when you stop working for a living your expenses go down tremendously. You aren't commuting any more, you don't wear the same quality of attire, and other things related to doing business also disappear, such as overhead on office space. Full retirement leads to a definite reduction in expenses. Of course, to retire in practice means you still have to cover some career-related expenses, which is why you also need to look at raising your passive income level if you want to be financially free.

We suggest you do the math on what you need to maintain your own lifestyle. Figure out what your expenses are, and then make a budget of how you plan to meet them. Once you start watching what you spend, you'll realize, "Oh I don't need this or that." By reducing your living expenses and assigning a higher portion of your income to your special accounts, you really can move to the level of financial freedom quicker.

Suggested amounts for a percentage split are:
- *Financial freedom*: 5 to 10 percent of gross
- *Taxes*: 20 to 30 percent of gross
- *Fun*: 3 to 5 percent after taxes
- *Debt reduction*: 10 to 20 percent after taxes
- *Bailout*: 10 percent after taxes
- *Expenses*: 25 to 50 percent after taxes

The Subconscious Takes It All In

When our eldest son, Josh, was very young, he would sit and play in the back of the room during our financial independence programs. He wasn't consciously paying attention to anything that was being said, but his subconscious mind was busily forming connections and forging brain pathways that had to do with money; basically he was taking notes and creating memories to be used at a future date. Fast forward several years to Josh's first paying job. After receiving his first paycheck, he innately knew that he wanted to separate his paycheck into percentages. Part of his paycheck went to a wealth account, part went to saving for the car of his dreams, and the rest was his "play" money. The interesting point is that we never had a conversation about what he should do with his paycheck. His mind automatically brought up that old memory.

Josh continued dividing his paychecks like this until by the time he went to chiropractic school, he was able to put a down payment on his first house! He and his wife, Meredith, continued this same practice after their wedding, and not long after he started in practice with Jay they were able to buy a bigger home in a beautiful, sought-after neighborhood!

Not only did Josh unconsciously learn about paying himself first with money, he also learned to pay himself in time. To this day, he takes time for himself and time with Meredith. He treasures those hours and it allows him to be totally present while he is in practice.

Reflection Question

If you achieved financial freedom, how would your life change? For instance, would you donate time and services to a free clinic, devote time to creating artwork, or travel more often? Your time is your most precious commodity—more valuable than money.

Get out a piece of paper and write down your thoughts about this question. Mull it over for a while. Have conversations about it with your friends and family members.

We have found this to be a highly motivating question. When we asked this question of ourselves, and of each other, we realized that we both wanted to travel the world. But we didn't want to spend much money to do it. Having identified a clear desire, however, Kathi decided to become a travel agent. This way we could travel for one-quarter of the price that the average person pays. Today, we have developed the means to travel more and to many more places every year as the average person does.

One of Jay's patients told him that he wanted to travel around the world. "You're not married and you have no kids who are dependent on you," Jay pointed out, asking, "What's keeping you here?" "Nothing," was his answer. Subsequently the man took a job on the cruise ship *Queen Elizabeth 2* and sailed the world. He was an actor and his job was performing for the passengers three nights a week. It was a perfect solution, one that lowered his expenses considerably even as he was living out his dreams.

Are you starting to understand how time and money often go hand and hand in our lives? To successfully retire in practice means you have discovered a way to have the ideal life you want while trading fewer hours for money. But there is a third ingredient in the being happily retired in practice recipe, and it's one nobody can afford to ignore: energy. For what good would it be to have enough time, but not enough energy to do the things you enjoy? And without sufficient energy to think clearly and work effectively, how can you make the most of the hours you do work to afford your leisure?

In the next chapter, "Keep Your Energy High," we'll look at the small, workable steps you can take to boost your energy and stamina, and win back your health (if you've lost it), or optimize your level of health, regardless of how healthy you think you are!

CHAPTER 3
KEEP YOUR ENERGY HIGH

"Happiness gives us the energy which is the basis of health."
—HENRI-FRÉDÉRIC AMIEL

We've already discussed changing how you manage your time and money. Those are both critical elements of the Retire in Practice (RIP) lifestyle. Having time and money will only serve you well when you have the third key. The third key to remaking your life to be a more meaningful and enriched life that you love—one in which you work to live rather than living to work—is *energy*. Let's focus now on how to improve the way you manage this third key element on a day-by-day basis.

The main reason for focusing on the care of your body is obvious: Your health and well-being are the foundation of everything you do. So you'll be glad to know that the health benefits of retiring in practice are numerous. Among other things, it:

- Reduces stress (which reduces chronic illness).
- Promotes longevity.
- Lessens anxiety and depression.
- Reduces belly fat (by lowering cortisol).
- Improves brain function.
- Builds self-worth.
- Increases the fun quotient in life.

Your body can never be divorced from your mind or emotions. The body-mind-spirit is a whole package, a networked system if you will. Thus, when you improve your physical well-being in any way, and to any degree, the betterment you obtain comes hand in hand with a handful of other highly desirable mental and emotional changes. Moreover, if you transform negative beliefs and attitudes into positive ones, this improves the health of your body and emotions. In other words, how you think also affects your well-being.

Jay gives a talk upon occasion in his chiropractic office called "Your Energy Is Your Life: The Five Pillars of Optimum Health, Vitality, and Longevity." He discusses five core ingredients: exercise, sleep and rest, nutrition, mental attitude, and maintaining a healthy spine and nervous system. In this chapter, we're going to go through each of these topics in turn, beginning with exercise.

Exercise: Use It or Lose It

At New York Chiropractic Life Center, we see clients whose bodies are degenerating at a younger age than they did twenty years ago. This is due to changes in our modern lifestyle that have to do with technology. People are playing virtual sports on the computer instead of real ones. They aren't working in offices anymore; they are telecommuting to work from their home offices. In their leisure time, they stay at the computer to play video games, surf the Internet, message their friends on social networks like Twitter and Facebook, or they are watching TV. As a result, it's as if people have gone from working a forty-hour week filled with movement and activity to a sedentary ninety-hour week. Adding insult to injury, staying seated a good part of the day and holding a static physical position reduces flexibility. In essence, our culture today lacks the component of routine physical activity that once was a part of helping people keep fit.

Think even of the difference between writing a letter on a computer and using an old-fashioned typewriter, where, as you came to the end of the page, you had to hit a lever to manually return the carriage to the right in order to start a new line of type. Even that one simple action required you to shift the position of your arm every minute or so. Now you never have to change the position of your hand. In the business world of the past you had to get up and walk around your office in order to step over to the copy machine, the filing cabinet, or the fax machine. You got out of your chair in the past; but now everything from printing copies, to saving files and sending faxes is done with a button right from where you are. As our work processes become more efficient and streamlined, our bodies are being robbed of movement that is necessary for our well-being.

We view health as a never-ending process that must be cultivated and maintained, and we look at illness as something to be prevented. We know that the human body will naturally heal itself if the right conditions are created for it to do so. Our role in health maintenance therefore is to remove obstructions to healing, which includes stepping in to provide that which is missing in the lifestyle that we typically lead these days. We need to stretch our muscles and soft tissues through our full range of movement. We need to do weight-bearing activities to maintain the strength of our bones and muscles. We also need to utilize the muscles of our hearts and lungs through aerobic activities to maintain their strength. So those are three main components of fitness: stretching, weight training, and aerobic activity.

That being said, all of this can be

> YOU WANT TO DIE YOUNG…AT A VERY OLD AGE!

accomplished in ways that you enjoy. We know one fifty-year old woman who gets her aerobic activity in by going out swing dancing, which she thoroughly enjoys—both for the movement and because she likes the music and the company. For ourselves, we like taking walks. It has been shown that people who take 10,000 steps a day are healthier than sedentary people, who average 3,000 or less steps per day. A distance of 2,000 steps is equivalent to a mile of walking. Ten thousand steps was the norm before the suburban automobile culture was born and computers came into vogue.

A research study at the University of Illinois at Urbana-Champaign led Dr. Arthur F. Kramer, reported in *Frontiers in Aging Neuroscience* (August 26, 2010), revealed that people who do an extra five miles of brisk walking every week—meaning that the pace speeds the heart rate a bit—have improved mental abilities for activities like planning, scheduling, handling ambiguity, as well as better memory and attention span. Walking is more beneficial for the brain than stretching or toning. The caveat is that you have to do it for at least a year. But it's worth it, especially for the elderly. According to Kramer and his team, walking even delays the progression of brain diseases like Alzheimer's.

If 10,000 steps seems like a lot to you, remember that just getting up and walking across the room and back counts as taking steps. Taking a break and walking around the block counts as taking steps. Walking up a flight or two of stairs instead of taking an elevator contributes to your total number of steps. And consider the benefits of taking a walk on your lunch break as part of your routine. Let your mind wander or invite a friend along to have a great conversation with you. Many of the steps throughout your day can be enjoyed. Plan to add more walking to your day in short increments.

In the RIP lifestyle, we advocate keeping things simple. If you prefer riding a bicycle to walking, swimming to biking, or dancing to swimming, understand that it's going to accomplish the same goal of improving your physical and mental health as long as the activity has an aerobic component. On a bike you push pedals. Swimming you push against and kick through the water. In all of these activities you are moving through a range of positions, bearing or pushing weight (your own body), and elevating your heart rate by placing a temporarily heightened demand on your heart and lungs. The same is true for jogging, tennis, bowling, and volleyball.

Remember, you don't have to come out of the gate like a race horse if your present level of fitness is low. Simply work your way toward more strenuous activity gradually and you will see regular effort rewarded over time. If you haven't been checked out by a doctor lately or think there might be an impediment to exercising, consult with your health professional before starting. Once you get the go-ahead signal, there is nothing to fear.

As for flexibility, we recommend that you plan to take breaks at intervals during the day to stretch and move around. In Japan, where people are notoriously devoted to their work, people are given stretch breaks throughout the day by their employers. No one is shamed for taking a break to stretch and move because everyone does it together.

Well, you can provide the same opportunity for yourself and your team of employees. Work for ninety minutes and then take a ten-minute stretch break.

If you or anyone on your team is experiencing repetitive stress injuries, such as everyday neck pain, back pain, or carpal tunnel syndrome from working too many hours in one position, put Handt's "rule of twenty" into practice: Stand up to reboot your brain every twenty minutes, and at the same time purposefully change something about your physical position. Put your legs up. Move your mouse pad two inches over or up and down. Alter the height of your chair. Or move either closer to, or farther away from your computer screen. If you pause every twenty minutes, you shift your position three times an hour.

The cure for the ills of the sedentary modern lifestyle is to become more active.

Sleep and Rest

Sleep is when the body restores, revitalizes, and regenerates itself. You can't possibly hope to remain healthy and feel energized during the day if you're not getting enough sleep at night. The human body has daily rhythms, which are coordinated with sunlight. When the sun rises, it shifts into a wakeful mode. As the night falls, it begins to shift into a resting mode. There is evidence that people who work on shifts that run counter to the cycle of daylight and nightfall put extra stress on their bodies because the pattern is unnatural.

Of course, everyone has an individual need for sleep. Some people need more, some less. And the amount a person needs is not always consistent. It depends on the level of activity that is pursued during the day, the amount of stress being experienced, and age. Children who are growing need more rest, as do the elderly. For those of us who are in the prime of life, it is best to respond to the signals of our bodies, which tell us when we need more sleep. If we feel fatigued, we need to sleep more. It's as simple as that.

"I usually take a two-hour nap from one to four."
—YOGI BERRA

There is no prescription for the right amount of sleep. In general, no two people require the same amount of sleep because no two people have the same body composition or live the same lifestyle. If you are constantly waking up before your alarm clock goes off, you may be scheduling yourself for too much sleep. Conversely, if you are constantly hitting the snooze alarm, you might not be scheduling enough sleep. You need to figure out your optimum sleep time and strive to achieve it as often as possible. Sleeping less than that on an ongoing basis and you will run a deficit. This isn't like taking a loan of hours that you can pay back to yourself on the weekend. You need to sleep regularly. In studies of sleep deprivation, it has been shown that people who are kept awake for even a few days begin to feel the impact in a reduction of mental and physical functioning. They even become a little delusional. If you've ever had insomnia, then you can probably relate to what this is like. Among other things, it's emotionally draining. Sleep itself has cycles within it. And it seems that we need to experience dream states and deep, dreamless sleep to feel well.

You can trust your body to let you know what it needs. If one morning you happen to awaken feeling fatigued, it means you need more rest. Should your schedule permit it, go back to sleep right then for another hour or two. If you have committed to be somewhere, make a plan to go to bed early that night. The sooner you can get some additional rest, the better you will feel. The body is self-restoring if we don't get in its way.

Also, consider taking a nap in the afternoon. Many people experience drowsiness mid-afternoon. This is independent of the consideration of what they ate for lunch. It is a natural lull in energy. Lying down for a twenty-minute nap and giving in to the impulse to rest can give you a second wind that will carry you through to bedtime. A NASA study of pilots showed that they were more alert and performed better in the later stages of flight if they had a brief nap midway through. There are many countries where the mid-afternoon nap, or siesta, is culturally embraced. It may only be the Puritan work ethic in America that makes so many of us feel as if we are shirking our duty if we lie down to nap. Many accomplished people in history, including Winston Churchill, Thomas Edison, and Albert Einstein, were avid nappers. It is important to note that the optimum nap time in order to avoid falling into a deeper sleep is twenty minutes. Remember, the purpose of the nap is to quickly super-charge and revitalize your mental and physical energy.

You can also get a boost of energy when you're feeling fatigued later in the day by doing light exercise. Exertion triggers the body to respond to meet the challenge. Of course, there is a balance to be struck. If you do too much exercise when you are tired, you'll feel worn out. Again, your body should let you know when enough is enough if you heed its signals. Stop exercising well before you reach exhaustion if your goal for the exercise session is to get a pick-me-up. Save pushing to the limit for fitness training.

In order to establish good sleep habits, it is recommended that you do as follows.

- Set a regular bedtime (9 P.M., 11 P.M., for instance) and stick to it.
- Begin winding down your activities an hour or two ahead of bedtime.
- Create non-disruptive conditions in your bedroom. Limit activities there to ones of quiet, relaxation, and comfort. Consider removing the TV set.
- Establish darkness. This is particularly important. If light shines on you from your window, consider installing "blackout curtains." If you have electronic devices that emanate light, such as a clock radio, either remove those devices or consider wearing an eye cover.

- Control the sounds you hear. Some people sleep better in the presence of "white noise," such as the sounds of the ocean or a rain forest. You can get a machine that creates soothing background noise. Alternatively, you may sleep better in silence. If you cannot eliminate ambient noise altogether, try earplugs.

In Chapter 1, "Take Your Life Back," we discussed the importance of incorporating intervals of leisure throughout your day. Taking regular vacations and long weekends off, as well as scheduling periodic breaks in your activity, is critical to how well you will function.

Nutrition

Nutritionally, the key to well-being is moderation. As far as we are concerned, you can eat anything you want diet-wise as long as you are not overeating. That being said, the healthiest people tend to eat a higher percentage of protein. But the form it comes in—whether it is from meat, fish, or beans and rice—is very much a personal choice. Protein contains the amino acids that are the essential building blocks of the body. Personally, we believe in keeping menus simple: We eat organic raw fruits and vegetables, lean meats, chicken, fish (for the omega-3 it contains), and eggs and do our best to stay away from white sugar, white flour, white salt (by contrast, red or pink salt contains vital minerals), and minimizing dairy intake. Refined and processed foods contain too many chemicals—preservatives, additives, hormones—for our liking. We are suspicious of genetically modified foods and therefore avoid eating them.

If you are overweight, you need to lose the weight. This can be done gradually, by skipping a couple of hundred calories a day while still maintaining sound nutrition. Face it: If you can't walk up a flight of steps without panting, you need to do something about your weight. If you are underweight, you need to gain weight by taking in extra healthy calories every day until you reach a healthy goal weight. The more activity you do, the more calories you need to eat. Go online and search for a BMI chart; this will give you a ballpark figure for what your appropriate weight and caloric intake should be for your age, gender, and height. You should be happy, and eating food you enjoy that is also healthy for you is part of living a good life.

Hundreds of books on different eating plans have been published. Cardiologist Arthur Agatston, M.D., wrote *The South Beach Diet* (Rodale, 2003), describing his program for heart healthy eating. Naturopath Peter D'Adamo, N.D., M.I.F.H.I., wrote *Eat Right 4 Your Type* (Putnam, 1996), explaining how to customize your diet for your blood type and genetics. Our favorite book is *The Wellness Prevention Paradigm* by James L. Chestnut, M.Sc.., D.C., C.C.W.P. (The Wellness Center—Global Self Help Corp, 2011). If you have any ongoing health conditions, like celiac disease or insulin resistance, it is best to ask for advice from your health care provider or a nutritionist on the appropriate plan for your individual needs.

The bottom line is that you need every component of nutrition—protein, fat, complex carbohydrates, fruits, and vegetables—because these nutrients are the fuel of the body. Carbohydrates are the quickest source of energy. Like liquid rocket fuel, they allow you to take off. If you need a sudden burst of energy, you can get it from eating carbs. But their energy also fades quickest. They burn off within two hours.

> "Create a definite plan for carrying out your desire and begin at once, whether you're ready or not, to put this plan into action."
> —NAPOLEON HILL

Protein and fat are more like solid fuel, because they sustain you over time. The body burns protein slower. It can sustain you for about four hours. Fat, which is an essential nutrient that you only need in smaller amounts, is even slower burning still: Its effects last about six hours.

When you're planning what to eat, think ahead in these terms: "Hey, when I get up I need a liquid fuel and a solid fuel. Three hours into the day, I will need another piece of fuel to give me an extra push. And three hours after that, another." You won't experience food cravings as long as your blood sugar stays level. To keep it level, figure you will need to eat every three hours—and combine proteins and carbs. At three o'clock, try an apple or banana with peanut butter. Eat six or seven small, balanced meals, starting with breakfast, and you won't have an energy crash. If your energy flags, you're likely to give in to the sudden, burning desire to consume a sleeve of cookies or a box of crackers. If you get a craving like this, eat a piece of fruit instead!

You also need to drink plenty of water. You might be surprised to know that even slight dehydration affects how well your brain works, and it lowers your energy. Keep a water bottle at hand and sip from it throughout the day. Water is essential.

Once you're into this regimen, it really feels good. Four to six weeks is all it takes to sense a noticeable change in your energy, moods, and mental functions. Try it out.

Mental Attitude

Once you take ownership of your time, you are going to feel more highly motivated and confident about everything you do. Meeting the goals that you set for yourself can be energizing and inspiring if you believe it is possible to accomplish them. Intimidating and draining, if you don't. Like most people who make lifestyle modifications, we expect you will start to see—usually in a very short period—that you are capable of doing much more than you ever imagined. Your sense of possibility will expand. But this only works if you have clarity about what you are doing every day and why it matters. Setting a goal that seems monumental is fine, as long as you can translate that into manageable, bite-sized pieces.

Holding a positive mindset, by the way, does not require you always to be happy and carefree. Rather it means that you have emotional resilience. You can allow yourself to feel your feelings and take care of yourself in ways that enable you to recover from sad and painful experiences, manage your challenges and frustrations, and enjoy mutually supportive relationships. The relatively new field of positive psychology studies people who are happy, successful, peaceful, compassionate, and resilient. It looks at qualities like optimism, creativity, and altruism. It focuses on how to create a good future. We can take some lessons from what they have learned.

One of the notable characteristics of high-functioning people is the way they talk to themselves. They don't call themselves names ("Dummy," "Slowpoke," "Fatso") or berate themselves for mistakes ("You never do anything right," "How could you be so stupid?"). They don't worry, "What will they think of me?" or "I need to catch up." Rather they encourage themselves ("You can do it!" "Hang in there, pal, you're doing everything you know how," "Next time you'll do better"). Their self-talk is loving ("You look great today," "You're such a good person," "Good job"). They focus on what goes right, instead of wrong. They learn from their mistakes, and don't dwell on the past.

> *"Think! Speak! Act! Positives!*
> *I Am! I Will! I Can! I Must!"*
> —B.J. PALMER, D.C.

High-functioning people take responsibility for the results they get in life, viewing themselves as capable and creative, rather than as victims of circumstance. And they look ahead. Negative self-talk is non-resourceful. It robs people of self-worth. Positive self-talk is resourceful. It lessens resentment and gives people energy for living well.

As a person who intends to retire in practice, to take control of your time, energy, and finances to make it possible to live an enriched and fulfilling life, having clarity about what you are doing and creating is essential. Daydreaming and purposefully visualizing what your ideal life will look and feel like can help. So talk about what you are creating, journal about it, or make a dream board—a collage of images symbolizing or displaying details of the life you intend to lead. These tools are useful for solidifying your vision of the future and ideal outcomes.

In their book *Your Money or Your Life* (Penguin, 1992), Joe Dominguez and Vicki Robin point out how we trade our lives for dollars. Specifically, if you earn $100 an hour, to buy a car for $10,000 you are trading one hundred hours of your life to own that car. Now think of how many hours of your life you would have to trade for a Mercedes, Porsche, and so on. When you have clarity about the time and energy cost of every purchase, it changes the way you make decisions. Are you willing to give up six hundred hours of your life to have a $60,000 car? When you buy things, always ask yourself, "Is this purchase going to add to the quality of my life in the long term or will it just give me instant satisfaction, a thrill that quickly wears off, leaving me wanting more?"

For ourselves, we would rather create a life where we are free to go to Mexico for a week or to take a ski trip rather than buying an expensive car to impress people. The excitement of newness wears off after a purchase. Knowing that a specific purchase is the equivalent of twelve days, three weeks, or two months of our lives gives us a real sense of what we're giving up to have the ownership of "stuff" we purchase. Because we're clear on our priorities, we think twice about what we spend money on, and also about what we need to do to have the things that we value, which are a priority to us.

The opposite is also true. If we know that we are working for something important, it motivates us to go after it actively. We can see that by putting in an extra ten hours of productive effort (rather than in reading joke emails or focusing on tasks that don't get us the greatest return on our effort), having what we want is within our grasp. Playing with finding new ways to have what we want has expanded our sense of possibility.

Flexibility is a key concept in our approach to business and life. Your level of flexibility determines whether or not you are able to preserve and bypass obstacles. If you aren't flexible, then there is only ever one way to do something; this limits your options. If you are flexible then you can achieve your goals by different methods; this expands your options. Years ago, we used to go skiing out West a lot. Our neighbor's dream for several years was to go skiing with us in Utah. He was saving up for it. Finally, he could afford to join us. Sadly for him, that was the only year Utah had no snow. We were able to switch our own reservations and go out to Colorado, which had snow that year. The airlines had no penalties for switching tickets back then. But he chose not to come because he was obsessed with the idea of "skiing in Utah." Unfortunately, our neighbor never made it to Utah and he died way too young without ever realizing his dream. His inflexibility about his plans and his inability to handle change made him miss some great Rocky Mountain skiing.

Nervous System Free of Interference

The final element in living a high-energy life is maintaining a nervous system that is free of interference. That's the focus of chiropractic care: to remove impediments to the messages that travel from your brain through your spinal cord and nervous system, and maintaining clear channels so that the body can heal itself. Every sign and symptom in the body is related to its mechanisms for survival. Learning to listen closely to your body therefore makes a big difference. Pay attention. Do you need to rest, to eat, to stretch, to blow off some steam in the gym, to seek some clarity, or to go out with friends and have fun? All those needs are being expressed through your nervous system. If you attend to your body's need to be unblocked, you'll find that you become and stay much healthier.

As you know, Jay is a chiropractor. We believe deeply in the philosophy of chiropractic and we have seen the remarkable benefits, both personally in our family and with people of every age, from infancy on up, who come to our office for everything from crisis care to optimum lifestyle care. A slip on the stairs, a car accident, too many hours seated in a stationary position before a computer screen, or unreleased emotions—all of these can be addressed and improved with chiropractic adjustments as well as keeping healthy people healthy. Then wellness is facilitated.

What's the purpose of the RIP lifestyle, if not to enjoy wellness and ease throughout your entire, hopefully long life? To ensure that you're around to enjoy your RIP lifestyle, we recommend that you read *The 100 Year Lifestyle* by Dr. Eric Plasker.

> IN CHIROPRACTIC, PHILOSOPHY, SCIENCE, AND ART ARE BRANCHES OF THE SAME TREE.

Do It in Baby Steps

From experience, we know that making change can seem daunting. If improving your health in some way—for instance, by getting fit, losing weight, or even learning and practicing unfamiliar life-enhancing skills—seems like a challenge right now, remember this: It's possible to do absolutely anything if you break it down into small steps. The idea is to be moving in the right direction. Then, even if you stumble on the path, you can only really fail if you quit. You can set yourself up to win in the long term by making a simple no-fail commitment to take care of your health in baby steps. The only difference between the possible and the impossible is that the impossible takes a little longer.

In his book *Influence* (HarperBusiness, 2006), social psychologist Robert Cialdini talks about what influences people to do certain things. How do you persuade someone, for instance, to donate bone marrow for transplantation? Donation can save a life, yet it is a major, painful procedure. He's found that if first you ask people to support the transplant foundation and give them a pin honoring them for it, and then ask them to be tested as a possible donor two weeks later, the compliance with such a request goes up astronomically. The first request was a baby step that influenced them to go to a deeper level of support and participation. In the same way, we can influence ourselves to do anything in the same way: bit by bit.

The first baby step of retiring in practice is to take some time off during the day. Promise to take at least an hour a day. This is time when you can sit down and read a book or listen to music for pleasure. Have a cup of coffee with a friend to get together and enjoy a relationship. Stroll in the park or through the neighborhood. In doing so, you take time back for yourself that your customer, employer, or family member otherwise would.

During this time, you can choose to do something not only to be "productive" or wealth building, but perhaps for your spiritual and personal growth. This is time for you to explore your passions and experience the revitalization of your soul.

Pick up the book *1,000 Places to See Before You Die* by Patricia Schultz (Workman, 2011). Read about three or four of these places and start marking off the ones you want to visit and ones you've already visited. Ask open-ended questions about what will give you the most pleasure and joy in life. Open-ended questions—as opposed to yes/no questions—give the brain a chance to search both inside you and in the world around you for answers. The kind of questions you ask about any issue, desire, goal, or dilemma will determine the outcome you get in your life.

This is not airy-fairy advice; when you give it a fair try, it can affect your longevity and improve your mental attitude, because it will support you in taking the steps you take. You deserve to have a good life and you deserve to treat yourself well. The better you treat yourself, the more energy you'll have for taking the steps towards your ideal life.

Call to Action: Make a Log of Everything You Do

Before changing anything in your habits, make a log of your current behavior so that you find out where your energy is being invested and identify energy-sapping patterns in your lifestyle. For at least one week, keep track of the following information.

- How often and how much do you exercise? What kind of exercise is it (for instance, stretching, jogging, weight training, biking, walking)? On a scale of 1–10, how intense is your effort (1 being no effort and 10 being so strenuous you can't keep going at that level for more than a minute or two)?

- How much sleep are you getting at night? Do you nap during the day? Does your energy drop at certain times of day? Are you taking relaxation breaks?
- What are you eating? Is it nutritious? What time of day do you eat? Do you get hungry between meals?
- Are you self-critical? Are you self-supportive? Do you blame? Are you resentful? Do you feel guilty or ashamed? How do you respond to negativity?
- Is your body displaying any symptoms of tension or pain? Have you made any plans to see a chiropractor?

Once a day, review your log and then ask this question: "If there was one thing I could do today to make myself feel better and raise my energy, what would it be?" As soon as you identify it, decide exactly what time it will be accomplished. Then do it.

The beauty of logging your behavior is that change will soon begin to happen just by increasing your awareness of energy sappers. You'll notice what feels easier or harder to modify, and where you need external support. In addition, you'll develop confidence in your ability to make changes, because you are doing it incrementally, but steadily. In a relatively short period, you will start to feel better physically, emotionally, and mentally, and you will want to go deeper into the process of change. You'll feel ready!

In the next chapter, "Build a Strong Team," we'll talk about another key way to get rid of energy sappers: developing an effective support system in your workplace.

CHAPTER 4
BUILD A STRONG TEAM

"Individual commitment to a group effort—that is what makes a team work, a company work, a society work, a civilization work."
—VINCE LOMBARDI

There are three ways to cut down on your work hours: delegation, automation, and deletion. In this chapter we're going to talk about delegation. A delegate is a person who's authorized to act on behalf of another. For instance, at The New York Chiropractic Life Center, Jay delegates bookkeeping to one staff member and social media activities to another. At her travel agency, Vacation on Your Mind, Kathi delegates the marketing of specialized tours to travel agents from the same demographic as the prospective travelers for each tour package (for example, a senior citizen running a marketing campaign for a seniors cruise or a college student marketing to college students taking trips for spring break). This frees us to focus on other activities. It's a way of time shifting.

When you delegate a task to a subordinate in your business, because you are entrusting that task to this team member, you have to be sure of two things: first, that the person has the ability to handle the task, or can be trained by you to handle it. When it's worth doing, it's worth being done well. Second, you need to know the person has the desire to handle the task, or the willingness to learn to handle it and take responsibility for his or her results. Without desire and willingness, there will be resistance and lackluster performance.

As for you, you need to be willing to let go of your ego ("Nobody can do this as good as me . . . or, God forbid, better!") and give away tasks to your team. Once your team is trained and you're confident in their ability to do the tasks you assign them, you can supervise them from the background. Be supportive without micromanaging. Micromanaging is the same as doing it yourself. Let them know they're not alone if they need your input. Offer oversight so they don't run amok. But empower them to take care of the job. Otherwise you could run into the problem of the person being frustrated by lack of ability, disempowered by your interference, or failing to perform adequately. Being a good people manager is a balance of hands on/hands off.

For the Retire in Practice lifestyle, the more tasks you can delegate to others the better.

Benefits You Can Expect from Delegation

There are several benefits of time shifting through delegation. These include:

- *Higher income*: Every day has the same twenty-four hours in it. Optimizing your day so you are focused on accomplishing the higher-earning actions in your business will increase your income. If you can pay someone a reasonable wage to handle tasks that would prevent you from servicing your customer or client in ways that require your specific expertise, then you are spending a little to bring in a lot more. The difference between the expense of paying someone and the new income can be calculated on your profit and loss sheets. High intake plus low expenditure equals profit.

- *More free time for "play-time" activities*: Having someone take over for you in the office liberates you to be elsewhere. Putting a strong team in place to help run your business is an essential component of the Retire in Practice lifestyle.

- *Peace of mind*: Business owners can easily fall prey to overwhelm and burnout. One of the most common complaints we hear from the people we coach is that they're working too hard and feeling overwhelmed by the number of tasks on their to-do lists. They know what to do, but don't feel like they have the time to get it done. As a result they try to do several things at once. Multitasking is a recipe for confusion and distraction. Those who delegate feel calmer, more relaxed, and have much greater clarity of mind than those who don't.

- *Happier employees*: The people who work for you need to feel challenged by what they do. Productive people matched with jobs that suit their strengths and personalities are happier when they're working than people doing the wrong jobs or jobs that bore them. It's like the story of *Goldilocks and the Three Bears*. Too little stimulation (the too-soft bed) and performance declines. Too much stimulation (the too-hard bed) and performance is impossible. A sufficient amount of stimulation (the bed that's "just right") and people come alive. Their performance is enhanced. They get excited to learn and grow.

Think of it this way. A few years ago, you may have loved doing some of the tasks you now want to give away. Your employees could feel the same. An ambitious young person following in your footsteps may look at these tasks as a career opportunity, a chance to develop a valuable skill set. A less ambitious person may simply appreciate the chance to utilize his or her talents for a purpose. There is satisfaction in a job well done. Delegation done right breeds loyalty, boosts morale, and reduces staff turnover.

Ideal Tasks to Delegate

What kind of tasks should you give away?

- Things you don't love doing. Remember this axiom: If you hate it, *donate it*.
- Things you're not competent to do. Nobody is good at everything. If you have a glaring weakness, that incompetence could become a liability. You're in business because you're a specialist of some kind. Let other people handle the things you haven't mastered or simply have no aptitude for doing. Some of the greatest minds and most successful people in history have said that they did not necessarily know how to do everything. They were geniuses at finding people who knew what they didn't. As Theodore Roosevelt said, "The best executive is the one who has sense enough to pick good men to do what he wants done, and self-restraint enough to keep from meddling with them while they do it."
- Things that you do not understand well. Confusion can lead to mistakes. Lack of comprehension simply means you need to ask for help.
- Repetitive or lower-level tasks. As the head of a team, you're in charge of the business vision (the big picture) and strategy (deciding what's important), oversight (checking the quality of the work done by the people you supervise), and offering specialized high-level service. Certain tasks have to be done on a daily or weekly basis to keep a business running smoothly—just not by you anymore.

• Things you like doing, but which you could give up in order to free more time to take care of things in your business that only you can do—or which you like doing more.

Given that you're committed to working less and playing more, to *retiring in practice*, the value of delegating is obvious. One way you can find the tasks to hand over to a subordinate team member, or to a specialist you bring in for this purpose, is to track your daily activities for a month. See what you actually do on a daily, weekly, and monthly basis. Write it down on a piece of paper. Add up the hours it takes you to do each one. Begin handing those tasks over one by one to delegates and watch your total hourly workload decrease before your eyes.

Who Are Your Ideal Delegates?

Of course, it's all well and good to advise you, "Delegate." But to whom? That's a very important question. Fortunately, in most instances, the ideal delegate could be any number of people. There are lots of different ways to handle delegation. Factors you'll want to take into consideration are whether the person is already employed by you or you need to hire someone for this purpose, how much money you want to devote to this specific purpose or function, and what kind of "bang" you want to get for your "buck." Talent. Money. Results.

Let's say you've decided you want to hand over the job of scheduling appointments to someone else. There are certain times of day when you are available to speak with clients on the phone or meet them face to face, and you've noticed that scheduling by phone and by email is taking you an hour a day. For

> *"We make a living by what we get. But a life by what we give."*
> —B. J. PALMER, D.C.

an hour-long phone consultation or appointment, you charge $100. Meaning, the hour of scheduling is robbing you of a potential $100. Nonetheless, scheduling is an essential task for the obvious reason that if you didn't schedule consults and appointments you would earn $0. Your dilemma is how to schedule effectively and at lowest cost to you.

Sure, you could automate your scheduling system (we'll discuss how in Chapter 5). But let's say you prefer the human touch in your customer service. You want people to have a good experience during this frontline scheduling process and feel welcomed. Perhaps you also want to screen your prospective clients to see if they're a good fit for you. Then, once you know they are suitable clients, you also want to do an assessment of their needs to prepare for the appointment or consultation. You're looking for an ideal delegate to handle this important role for you in your business.

The first thing you need to do is write a job description—for the sake of clarity—that covers what actually must happen during phone calls to schedule clients. For this example, let's say the job is simple: the phone rings, someone in your office (or at a remote location) must answer it by saying the name of your business, this person then must look into your calendar, find openings, and negotiate with people on the other end of the line to put them in the soonest available spot. You also want this person to capture the telephone number and email address of the caller, so that confirmation emails and reminders ahead of the appointment can be sent, or rescheduling and cancellation can take place, if that's ever necessary.

The second thing you need to do is to determine the skills and qualities of the person who could accomplish the features of your description in an ideal way. Let's say you most of all want your delegate to speak clear, proper English (and/or another language), to be friendly and cheerful, and also to be a patient listener. This person must also be competent on the Internet.

Now you look around for the right person. Is it someone you already employ who can perform this task in addition to what he/she already does? Do you need to hire someone new?

Go down the following list of assessments whenever you need to delegate a task. The ideal delegate is someone:

- Who loves to do the task and will apply his/her own creativity to accomplishing it well.
- With the right aptitude and personality for the task.
- With appropriate training or specialization, such as a certified public accountant, a writer, a search engine optimization expert, a licensed health care provider, a professional [fill in the blank].
- You trust to do it properly with minimal supervision.

When you've found an appropriate person, you can delegate the task with assurance. At The New York Chiropractic Life Center, one staff member is great at patient relationships, but hates doing record-keeping on the computer. She works at the front desk alongside another woman who formerly ran her own store and no longer wanted the responsibilities of owning a business. This second staff members likes doing the bookkeeping. Our son, Dr. Josh Handt, and daughter, Dr. Morgan Handt, who see their own patients, also cover Jay's patients when we're away on a trip. Our team has been working together for several years and functions now like a well-oiled machine.

How to Assess People's Aptitudes

The thing to keep in mind is that everybody has a specialty. When they find that specialty, they excel at it. It might not be something they've identified yet. But you can help them. As a business owner, part of your job is to fit other people to their jobs by discovering their passions and strengths. You can accomplish this, first and foremost, by using the Socratic Method of talking to them at length and asking lots of questions. In addition you can rely upon personality profiling tests, *psychometric* assessments like the Myers-Briggs Type Indicator, which ranks people on a scale of extroversion/introversion, sensing/intuition, thinking/feeling, and judgment/perception. An ENTJ type would be an extroverted, intuiting, thinking, judging person with an aptitude for certain job assignments that an ISFP (introverted, sensing, feeling, perceiving) person would not—and vice versa. Teams benefit inordinately from having members with different aptitudes and skill sets.

Neuro-linguistic programming (NLP) is another interesting tool for assessing people. Basically, our brains are "hardwired" through the way the networks of neural pathways—and hence the thought patterns—are set up to give us dominant modes of perception. We are going to discuss the four major modes. There are *visual* people, for whom sight is the dominant mode of experience; *auditory* people, for whom hearing is the dominant mode; *kinesthetic* people, for whom feeling/sensation is dominant; and *auditory didactic* people, who are analytical (they hear a voice running commentary inside their heads—and it's not a hallucination or God speaking to them). Where the linguistic part of the equation comes in is that people who are visual typically use visual words to describe things: "I *see* what you mean," "It's *clear* to me." Auditory people say things like, "It *sounds* like you're upset," "It *rings* a bell." Kinesthetic people might say, "I *catch* your drift," "It *felt* like the right choice."

When you sit down face to face and speak with someone for any length of time, you can easily determine if they're extroverted or introverted, not only through their demeanor—looking you in the eyes, open body language, approaching you first at a party—but also through the adjectives and adverbs they use to describe things they do. For instance, a young guy who doesn't like people much and loves to play around on computers might be ideal to input data. His personality type is introverted. If his sensory mode is *auditory didactic*, he might excel at calculations as well.

A woman who sees the world brightly and has a bubbly personality is an extrovert. If her sensory mode is *visual*, she might be ideal in a reception area, where she can oversee the activity of people coming and going. If her sensory mode is *auditory*, she might love making phone calls.

Kinesthetic people tend to be empathetic because they are able to feel what others feel. They excel at jobs that involve human interaction or where movement is involved.

If you learn that someone is active in sports or reading, or watches a lot of movies, or listens to the radio nonstop, then you've learned something about this person's personality that can be factored into your job delegation and hiring decisions.

By the way, it's not a bad idea to reassign people to different roles from time to time so they can learn more aspects of running your business. Not only does this mean they can cover for someone who is absent, it also gives them an appreciation for what their teammates do well. In the car industry, research showed that people performed better if they were given a new job assignment every six months or so. The challenge stimulated and engaged them.

Personal engagement is critical to success in any endeavor, and this comes from having a vision and meaningful purpose. Bill Gates, the founder of Microsoft, had a

> "Never tell people how to do things. Tell them what to do and they will surprise you with their ingenuity."
> —GEORGE S. PATTON

vision of putting a computer in every household in America. Now he and his wife Melinda are passionate about a vision of using their wealth to help humanity. Mark Zuckerberg, the guy who built Facebook, was passionate about finding new ways to connect people online. Warren Buffett, the CEO of Berkshire Hathaway, gets up and does what he does—guiding people in their investments—for philanthropic reasons. It's not about the money; it's about making people's lives better.

Are you familiar with the 80/20 rule? Eighty percent of your income comes from 20 percent of your activities. The same is true for your staff's activities. The 20 percent of staff members who are most engaged will deliver 80 percent of the results. We've found that people who are the most passionate about making a difference in people's lives do the best work for us, so we aim to help them develop a vision that's bigger than they are. They need a reason for doing what they are doing on a daily basis that's greater than self-gratification or their pocketbooks alone. It doesn't matter if someone is earning twenty, thirty, or forty grand a year. Every member of our team has told Jay that they love what they do. Though they could do it elsewhere and possibly earn more money, they love working here.

Forget about team members that show up just to get a pay-check—they don't feel a sense of purpose or passion about what they do. They won't contribute much to your success. If you can engage them, keep them. But if not, axe the dead wood as soon as you can.

Years and years ago, everyone in the office was complaining incessantly. It got so out of hand that we thought, *This is ridiculous! We're not having a good time.* We decided to fire everybody and start over with a new set of people. That shakeup positively changed the course of our business and led to much better results. By the same token, we firmly believe in rewarding people by showing our appreciation when things go well. We believe in acknowledgment.

Offer Clear Supervision

So you've delegated a task. Tell the employee: "This is the outcome we are looking for. These are the results we want to achieve. This is the direction we're going in, and these are the steps to guide you along the way. Once you appreciate all of this and understand the basics of this project, we encourage you to infuse your own magic, creativity, and personality into it to make it your own. " That works really well.

Give your people enticements for doing a good job: an extra day off, a bonus check, a gift, public acknowledgment (and often the best reward is a surprise reward!)—things they'll personally find rewarding and enticing. Challenge and involve and engage them. Ask them for their suggestions on how to accomplish a goal, such as bringing in a hundred new clients. Say, "How do you think we can get there?" That makes the whole office feel a part of the same mission. When the team's ideas work, invite them up to the house for a pool party, a holiday party, or take them out for lunch. They'll feel like a family.

The Peter Principle is the idea that a person rises to the level of their incompetence. So your role is to figure out how to exploit the magic within every person to bring them to their fullest potential. Keep raising the level of their competence. Hold staff meetings once a month, every two weeks, or even every week, and don't wait for an annual review. Ask, "What do we need to do to improve this?" Not you or me . . . *but us together?*

Who Is Minding the Store When You're Not?

As a doctor of chiropractic, like Jay, you need an associate or partner who provides patient care similar to the way you do. And you need the loyalty of this associate, so you can delegate patient care to them with full trust when you're away. When we go of town, Jay knows that Josh and Morgan are doing the right things back at the office, including handling paperwork (billing, insurance, charts) and seeing patients. Nothing changes much whether Jay is in or out. Jay even likes to joke, "The office runs better when I'm not there."

One of our closest friends has an associate-driven chiropractic practice. Sharon supplies support staff and space, and handles the business end of things, while a team of doctors care for the patients. She lives in Atlanta now and her Pennsylvania practice is thriving! She became successful by making sure the docs she hires love what they do, establishing a lucrative bonus system, paying well, and making sure before hiring new team members that they think the way she thinks about chiropractic care. She is passionate about chiropractic care. She also loves the energy, excitement, and challenge of starting a new practice and she's done it very successfully several times.

Both Sharon and Jay appreciate the necessity of training a new doc and having them buy into the vision of the practice. This prep time with new associates is one of the best investments you can make in growing an associate-driven practice.

We're good friends with Guy F. Riekeman, D.C., the president of Life University, where Jay is on the board of trustees. What makes Guy great at what he does is that he transfers his vision to the people around him. He finds people whose abilities complement his own and then leads them to pursue the same vision. Sole proprietors often think, "No one can do this as well as me," and then the business falls apart due to their blind spots. By contrast, Guy surrounds himself with people who excel at their specialties! That's a strong approach to running a business.

From time to time most business owners need to bring in efficiency experts and advisors. But it's also important to build a team of solution-oriented people around you. Tell your people: "If you come to me with a problem, also come with a possible solution to fix it." That gives your team the challenge of initiating a productive conversation with you—a true starting point for change.

When you're out of town, you have a choice either to check in at regular intervals or to have the person left in charge contact you (by phone, email, text, carrier pigeon). But really, how can you solve their problems from far away? What purpose would their calls serve other than giving them an opportunity to complain? We believe it's better to let them know they have the responsibility and the authority to do what needs to be done to fix problems. Put an office manager in place who can act as the "head honcho" while you're gone. This person should be tasked with overseeing the other staff members and ensuring that they adhere to your vision—and be empowered to make decisions.

Delegating when you are there and when you're away is essentially the same proposition. Meeting the responsibility of a position that you entrust them with is your staff's job. Rather than constantly looking over their shoulders, empower them to manage themselves. Otherwise you'll have two people doing the same work: them and you. The idea is to find someone who takes ownership of a given assignment and not remain immersed in it on a daily basis. In Jay's office, he knows the work is getting done properly. If there's a question on a patient being handled by another doctor, he can always peer into an exam room and offer a quick consult.

Outsourcing as a Mode of Delegation

In some businesses, like Jay's, where clients need to be seen in person, there has to be a professional office space and an onsite support team. In other businesses, like Kathi's home-based travel agency, a sole proprietor works with clients over the phone and by computer. Many people in Kathi's position now work remotely with a virtual assistant (VA). VAs can schedule clients, pay bills, do research, and update your website, as well as a host of other tasks, if they have the right skill set for it. The benefit of virtual assistance is to reduce overhead expenses like paying payroll taxes, site insurance, vacation days, and workers' compensation.

Other than the primary service you provide, you could outsource everything. All other jobs that need to be done to effectively operate both types of businesses—those with office space and those without—can be outsourced, including:

- Accounting.
- Marketing.
- Production.
- Publicity.
- Newsletters.
- Answering the phone.
- Scheduling.

The real decision that needs to be made when choosing to outsource is whether to hire an individual or a company that provides the services you require.

When you subcontract services to individual providers that do something similar as you, you're generally dealing with individuals. You must form a specific contract with them to pay them on an hourly, a weekly, or a monthly rate, on completion of a project, or on commission for sales brought in. Kathi, for instance, has hired other licensed travel agents strictly on commission with a favorable split to help her tap into specific markets: a senior citizen to reach out to the senior market, a college student to promote tour packages for college spring breaks, and so on. We also know an editor who subcontracts work to other editors and pays them a flat rate.

One motivational speaker hired a virtual assistant to manage her operations who has a built-in financial investment in the success of her business. Her VA receives a monthly flat rate along with a commission for every speech she helps the speaker book. The VA works exclusively with the speaker and only four other clients. She's a high-level performer with creative ideas and opinions about promotional strategies that have contributed to the speaker's success.

At The New York Chiropractic Life Center, we outsource the processing of insurance claims to a company that specializes in this service. The company we use has staff members who are available to us daily, so we know that even if one person falls ill or has a family emergency, the work continues being done on a timely basis. And if there's ever an issue with a claim it can be straightened out right away. We outsource our newsletter to a company that prepares a customized newsletter for us and then handles the bulk mailing of it to our clients. We outsource the promotion of our website to a search engine optimization (SEO) provider. But our support team handles personalized customer service in our offices, as we believe in the human touch.

When you choose to outsource different tasks, someone inside your business has to be designated to be the point person, acting as the liaison to the service provider. That could be you or one of your in-house team. It's important to monitor the quality of outsourced efforts. The more intimately connected a provider is to your business, such as a VA or a subcontractor would be, the more they must function as a member of your entire team. The quality of their work reflects on your performance with your clients and customers.

In this day and age, when so many things are handled through automation and by computer, you have more choices available of which companies to outsource to. So if the job is not being done effectively, do not hesitate to switch providers. You have plenty of options.

Once you put a strong team in place, both inside your office and outside your office, then you can comfortably enjoy the flexibility, leisure, and pleasures of the Retire in Practice lifestyle.

Reflection Questions

Ask and answer the following questions.

- How does your team stack up? Can you delegate and walk away?
- Does your team understand exactly what is expected of them?
- What's your trust quotient? How much do you trust the people around you to allow them to do what they need to do?
- Is your trust based on your team's competence?
- Is your lack of trust based on your team's incompetence?
- How might you clarify your agreements with your team members to increase your level of trust in their capabilities when you delegate?

Call to Action: Make a Delegation Plan

There's no time like the present to get started delegating. Based on everything we've discussed in this chapter, you're probably clear now on the types of tasks to hand over to support personnel—either team members on your staff who work alongside you in your practice or outsiders to whom you outsource different projects and responsibilities.

Begin by reviewing the list of "Ideal Tasks to Delegate" earlier in this chapter. According to these parameters, select some tasks from your own business that you could delegate and would appreciate delegating to someone else. What are three to five items on your list that you could delegate in the next week or month? We encourage you to set your ego aside (the little voice in your head that tells you, "No one can do this as well as me") and stretch. Delegate at least one task you feel uncomfortable delegating.

Refer back to the reflection questions at the end of Chapter 1. Which one task, if you delegated it, would free up the most amount of time in your day or week? Are there tasks in a particular area of your life where you need more balance that you could delegate immediately or in the next month? If you prioritize assigning these responsibilities to someone else, you'll liberate time and energy better employed for other pursuits.

With your list of three to five items in hand, quickly decide who you'd like to handle each task for you, and then notify that individual or service. Don't hesitate to act on your plan. You won't regret it. This step has the potential to change your life dramatically.

After you've made your delegation plan, read on. Our next topic is automated systems. As a complement to delegation, automation can be a very efficient and cost-effective way of streamlining your business and reducing your work load.

Chapter 5
Use Automated Systems

"Life doesn't have to be so damn hard."
—Timothy Ferriss

Cutting down on your work hours and streamlining your processes can be accomplished very effectively with automation. Automation can occur both inside and outside the office, through online systems that exist in the virtual world of networks accessed by computer. Many times automation is also a feature of outsourcing business activities to other human beings. In addition, it offers advantages to teammates, like file sharing and co-creation from remote locations.

For automation to be a profitable choice, the return on your investment in any automated system must be greater than the income you make in the time the system saves you. Pay less and earn more. You know the formula is working perfectly if your automated system does its job efficiently, gets you the results you expect and want, is user-friendly, helps you avoid mistakes and hit deadlines, and saves you time and energy. Inside your office, automation can be used to manage your cash flow, taxes, and payroll, organize and analyze your records, and supervise your calendar.

One of the greatest benefits of Web-based automated systems is that they can be accessed by you and your customers or clients

24/7 from any location. Among other things, automation can be used to communicate, generate sales, process payments, and schedule appointments. Though it does not substitute for good customer service provided by you and your staff when the human touch is necessary or preferred, in our high-tech society it is a basic feature we expect from the businesses we go to. By not automating certain functions, you'd lag behind your competitors.

Let's look first at the simplest thing.

Automate Your Calendar

Set up an automated calendar for the benefit of your team and for your clients. This could show when your office will be open and when it will be closed for a holiday or a special event. It could show when and where you are lecturing. By automating the calendar, it changes anytime someone with the right access code inputs new or revised information. In this way, it will always be up to date with correct information and serve as a central hub for your staff to refer back to.

If you use an automated online scheduling service, like Time-Trade.com, you can give your clients the option of choosing a convenient time for an appointment, which you have the right to confirm or deny by email. This means they can schedule whenever they think to do so, even at times of day or night or on weekends when your office is closed.

Automated Phone Systems

Voicemail is an obvious advantage for a business. If a live person is not available to answer the phone, a recorded voice can explain your office hours and take messages, letting callers know you value them and will reply at the earliest opportunity.

If there are a number of people on staff for whom a call might be directed, you can set up a phone system to direct people to different extensions by punching the right number option on their touchtone phone. We believe there should always be a "0" option to connect directly with a live person if you do this. Being unable to get a person on the line can frustrate callers.

Automate Your Financial Programs

From Day 1 in business, you need to set in place a good accounting system. Software programs now exist for bookkeeping that you can use to manage your cash flow, your taxes, your payroll, and everything else of a financial nature. A program like this can save you hours of time formerly spent in compiling the information you need when your tax payments and tax forms are due, and even completing those forms on your behalf. We recommend you use an accounting program capable of this even if you're only setting aside withholding taxes for one person.

The important point is that as long as the information entered into the system by you or someone else is up to date and accurate, the output from the system will be correct. It is automated; nonetheless there is an ongoing human component to making it function.

Whichever accounting system you choose should be a system that can grow along with you in complexity as your business expands in size and in scope. Many people start out using Quick Books, for instance, and upgrade late to QuickBooks Pro. The Pro version includes an option for tax preparation. Periodic accounting becomes very easy with QuickBooks, as it can translate financial records into spreadsheets that are simple to read and understand. It can even be used to manage inventory. Another good thing is that most bookkeepers know how to interface with this software, so if you lose one bookkeeper the next can rapidly get up to speed with your data.

One beauty of automated accounting is programming a system to send you reminders prior to the dates that certain payments are due to be made, giving you sufficient warning. It can also track outstanding payments you are owed, so you can circle back and generate reminders.

You can use automated accounting to:
- Monitor your profits and losses.
- Coordinate your banking.
- Handle your billing.
- Calculate accounts received.
- Manage your inventory.
- File insurance claims.
- File taxes.
- Write checks
- And more.

Nobody loves paperwork, so the way you do your paperwork needs to be as simple and streamlined as possible. There also needs to be oversight of how it's being handled to ensure that errors aren't being made. Whoever inputs data needs to do so correctly, and no one is perfect.

The hardest part of using automated accounting systems is the initial phase of setting them up. You have to be careful in naming the line items you want to track. For instance, where does your income flow from: consults, courses, product sales, or affiliate programs? And where does your income flow to? What categories do your expenses fall under: rent, salaries, equipment, office supplies, insurance, taxes as well as your various savings accounts? The more specific the categories, the better you can see where your money is going, thus giving you a much clearer picture of your financial health. Once the system is set in motion, for the most part you won't need to do anything other than input new data and generate reports. The more specific, clear, and accurate you are in the setup phase, the more headaches you can avoid later on. Then its click, click, click. Maintain.

We recommend doing an audit of your automated systems quarterly. When they come up for review, think carefully about how things are set up and make adjustments. Your business may have grown, so you might need to think about what you're doing differently.

Automated banking is an outsourced system that can be a big time saver. Almost everyone uses online banking today, though not always to its fullest capacity. Because of devices that can scan checks, as well as input credit card information, going to the bank in person is rarely needed today. Utility bills (heating, water, electricity) and phone bills can be paid directly online. You can even have checks mailed directly from your bank at your instruction when this is needed.

The important caveat here is to remember to record all banking transactions that take place online in your accounting program. If you don't do this diligently and accurately on a regular basis you can lose track of your cash flow in and out of your bank accounts.

At The New York Chiropractic Life Center, we choose to outsource insurance claims to a specialized service, but a staff member monitors to ensure that billing is being properly managed. We track the work our insurance handlers are doing for us in our automated accounting system. Annually we reflect on whether to renew our contract with this service provider or switch to a different one. If we weren't happy, we would switch in a heartbeat.

Your Financial Advisory Team

Business owners benefit from working with advisers they can call upon when needed. These professionals can prevent you from mistakes at setup. Advisors you need access to include:

- A financial or investment adviser.
- A legal adviser.
- Mentors, like volunteers from the U.S. Small Business Administration resource SCORE (see Score. com), or someone in your profession whom you trust.
- Insurance advisers that can help you set up the right coverage, possibly including unemployment insurance, workers' compensation, property liability for things like trips and falls, flood insurance, professional liability, and errors and omissions insurance. The kind of insurance you require for your business depends on the type of business space you use and the type of service you provide.

If you have been in business for a while, but your accounting systems are not yet automated, we believe setting up an automated system will be a breakthrough for you. We have a close friend who has been in practice for forty years. For a long time there was no bookkeeping at all in his business. He was working on a cash basis and wasn't accepting insurance or credit card payments, so he would just shove the money his clients paid him into his pocket. At the end of the day, he would bring the cash home with him in a garbage bag. One time he accidentally threw a bag full of cash out the window of his car into a dumpster thinking it was garbage.

Our friend started creating bookkeeping ledgers, which considerably improved his ability to manage his finances because it was easier for him to predict where certain expenses would occur during the year as well as track the balance of his profits and expenses. Even so, this was time consuming for his secretary, who had to post every item in the ledger by hand.

Ultimately he invested in a good computer and accounting software, and brought his business up to date in terms of banking, credit cards, and insurance. This made his secretary's job easier and freed her up to do other tasks. An important benefit of automation for him was that he started putting 10 percent of his receipts into his account on a daily basis. Then his Wealth account grew.

Remember, two of the most important accounts you can set up for yourself if you are running an independent business are a Wealth account and a Tax account (see chapter 2). You can get behind the eight ball if you are not prepared for estimated taxes and if you don't save money for your future.

Websites and Online Shopping Carts

Every business today benefits from having a presence online. This is a virtual hub that, like your actual office, is a center for your customers and clients to interact with you. It's a home base where they can find out more about your credentials, your services, and the products you sell. Depending on the nature of your business, features on the website can include everything imaginable, from scheduling appointments to announcing events; supplying downloadable reading materials, podcasts, and videos; and products that you hold in physical inventory.

A website is both a marketing tool, like a brochure would be, and a literal storefront. If you link your website to an online shopping cart you can take payments 24/7 from customers and clients for a variety of goods and services. You can also use the automated systems built into the online shopping cart to send out one-time email blasts or a series of scheduled messages, known as auto-responders.

Let's say you decided to offer a sale on a particular product. You could send out a message informing your entire mailing list of the sale with one push of a button. The system would add a greeting line personalized to each individual the message goes out to: "Dear Bob," for example, or "Dear Susie."

Or let's say that once you've sold a product, you want to follow up with your customers. You could set up a series of messages that are automated to be emailed to clients seven days, thirty days, and ninety days after a sale takes place. If Bob buys his product on January 1, he receives a message on January 8, January 31, and so on. If Susie buys her product on January 5, she receives a message on January 12, February 4, and so on. Those auto-responders are programmed at time intervals rather than on specific dates, like a single message would be programmed.

Back at your office, you can set up the system to send you an email alert whenever a product is sold. If you are holding the product in physical inventory, this would trigger you to take action to package and ship it—or to alert a fulfillment center to fulfill the order. You can use the alert as a trigger to take any kind of action that is appropriate to your business model. Many people sell services through online shopping carts.

Popular online shopping carts include: 1ShoppingCart.com, InfusionSoft.com, and AWeber.com, among others. These services can be purchased by month or by year, and most offer a discount for a trial period so that you can play around and see if they suit your needs. Some online mailing systems, like iContact and Constant Contact, offer auto-responders without shopping cart features, but can be linked to a cart.

Another great feature of online shopping carts is that you can set them up to take repeated payments from the customer's credit card (with the customer's approval). You might set up a three-pay option for someone in order to tempt them to buy an item that would be beyond their reach if they had to pay for it all at once. Some trainers and coaches have continuity programs where students pay on a month-by-month basis only as long as they want to participate. Other people set up membership sites, where membership needs to be renewed at intervals.

When you build a website for your business, think carefully about your physical activities and see if you can offer a virtual counterpart to them. Also think carefully about the needs of the consumer you are targeting. Perhaps there is something you can offer to them online that goes beyond your in-person services. The beauty of websites is that they can be built with links and buttons in them that instantly transport those who visit them to other online locations. This capability means you can affiliate yourself with stores, service providers, schools, libraries, and more. You can earn income through affiliate marketing efforts.

You can also install "Share" features on your website that enable visitors to follow you on social networks, like Facebook, Twitter, 4Square, and LinkedIn, and also to send out messages to their contacts suggesting they come and visit your website like they did.

If you build a website, it's a good idea to hire a search engine optimization (SEO) expert to set up links throughout the virtual space of the Internet that drives traffic to your website. Rather than learn how to do this on your own, outsource this to someone for whom this kind of activity is a passion. It takes a special kind of brain to do SEO well.

A website needs to be more than aesthetically pleasing. It has to get you results: clients and product sales. Thus, analytics are an important feature of professional website design. Analytics help you keep track of where your customers come from. If you don't know if someone came to you from a Google Ad or the Yellow Pages, you really have no idea what is and is not working.

We have found that more educated clients are coming in since we put up our first website. They say, "I researched you, and this is why I picked you. Yours is a family practice . . . you have years of experience . . . and so on." Whatever it is that they are looking for, the website has pre-sold them on our services. They begin by going to a directory, like Google, Yahoo, or Bing, and searching for a specialist in New York City. When they find a list, they often narrow the search down to our neighborhood, put in "chiropractor," and see our ratings. If they like the general information, they read the site and choose to contact us from seeing what's there.

Automate Your Online Social Networking

Many businesses today are marketed through Web-based social networks, like Facebook, Twitter, and LinkedIn. The more prominent these have become—meaning, the more popular they are among a variety of users—and the more sophisticated their technology has become, including how integrated they are with other systems and applications, the more valuable they have the potential to be for your business. A main reason for this is that they enable users to target their messages to specific populations.

Until recently, participating in social networking was a time-consuming activity. It still can be. However, a number of automated support systems now exist that make it possible to queue your messages for future posting at a specific date and time. This has really cut down on the frequency with which we have to go on the social networks live.

If you believe your intended customers or clients are participating in the online social networks and you believe this would be a good place for you to reach out, then go ahead and set up an account with a congregator, like Hootsuite.com or Socialoomph.com. It will save you oodles of time and give you better analytics of your followers. Such systems have free versions, as well as "pro" or "premium" plans, so they're affordable.

Automate Your Newsletters

Staying in touch with your customers periodically through a newsletter is a good strategy. We prefer to mail a printed newsletter on a quarterly basis for our practice members. Some people send out email newsletters. We do that as well. We now hire a company that produces a newsletter for us that includes health-related articles and customized features related to our practice, and also handles the bulk mailing of the newsletter to the people on our mailing list.

Years ago, before switching to the newsletter service, and even before personal computers, half a dozen friends—all chiropractors—would produce a newsletter together. One was in Michigan. One was in Florida. One was in California. We were in New York. First, we would type up a newsletter, which we mailed out to our own clients. Then we would trade newsletter content and repurpose it. For six months or so, we would cut and paste articles taken from the others' newsletters and customize them for our own needs. We printed 500 copies in a copy center and folded and stamped them by hand. It was a laborious process. It took us two days alone just to type up the labels we stuck on the newsletters.

When we initially started buying the newsletter, the printers would print 2,500 for us, but we still did the labeling ourselves. With the computer, of course, this was faster. But putting on the labels and stamps took hours. Now our mailing list is larger and we pay the service to do everything (outsourcing is wonderful and time saving!). They print the newsletters, address them, and mail them. Even though we could switch our outreach entirely to email newsletters, we believe getting something you can hold in your hand is more memorable and personal than an email, which you can delete with a click. Our practice members are much more likely to read the printed version!

We always personalize the messages we send to our practice members. We never send out an email or a newsletter to a generic person, "Dear Customer." Instead we make sure to use a person's first name, "Dear George."

If we take a phone message and say we're going to respond within forty-eight hours, we do. We actually try to respond quicker than we promise. Over delivery on promises is our policy. There is no faster way to lose a customer's trust than breaking a promise you made.

In marketing there is no substitute for extraordinary customer service and the human touch. There is no substitute for authentic caring. When we give a gift, it is a real gift of a service, not a discount on the price of the next service they buy. Our gifts are not enticements, but real gifts.

Things You Should Never Automate

In a doctor's office, going over the results of tests and reporting positive or negative findings should always be done in person or by phone, and never by email. If financial matters are being discussed, this should be done one on one, too, as money is also a personal subject.

We don't automate birthday greetings. We send out personal letters hand addressed to our patients, which tells them significant events that have happened throughout history on their birthdays. We get a huge response for these letters, which are also signed by hand. Of all we do, it is the thing we do that perhaps gets us the greatest results; more than any other form of marketing. And it's funny...though the letter doesn't change year after year, people still love it.

We also make a point to mail out cards of appreciation and acknowledgment. If we know, for instance, that someone's grandson is graduating elementary school, we send a card. Or if someone in the family passes away or gets married, we send a card. During appointments we are listening to the details of our patients' lives, so we like to acknowledge them in an unexpected way. Cards let them know we genuinely care about them and cultivate patient loyalty.

In your own business, you will have to figure out the right mixture of automation and personal attention you give your customers and clients. Automation and outsourcing can free your time up so you can give them the attention they want and deserve when it matters most, and can help make it more convenient for them to interact with you and purchase from you 24/7.

Call to Action: Set up an Automated System

If you could automate one activity in your business, which would free up the most time and the most mental and emotional energy for you or your staff? Which would help your business become more profitable? Which could generate passive income?

In the next week to a month, we challenge you to identify one area of your business that could be automated, choose an appropriate system to accomplish this goal (you may need to do a little comparison shopping), and then get that automated system set up.

You and your team may have to adapt and adjust to working with the system, and assuredly someone in your business will have to become responsible for maintaining it. However, once the initial hurdles and hiccups are overcome, we believe you'll wonder how you ever lived without automation in this particular area.

Tip: Evaluate this decision after a month or two to see if you are making full use of the system's potentials. Be sure to take advantage of your system's training modules.

~

In this chapter, we've been looking at ways of using technology innovatively to collapse time, getting more done with less time and effort. In the next chapter, we'll look at ways of using technology to collapse distance—getting more done *from further away*.

CHAPTER 6
LONG-DISTANCE PROGRAMS

"Invisible threads are the strongest ties."
—FRIEDRICH NIETZSCHE

For the Retire in Practice lifestyle, an ingenious way to time shift is to develop long-distance programs. When you can do your work remotely, either from home during the workweek or while away on vacation, then you can cut down on travel time, reach a significantly greater number of people (boosting your income), and enjoy yourself more. Working in the comfort of your own home or of a vacation spot is made possible by an explosion of online networks and devices. This chapter is about nontraditional ways of providing services using new forms of technology that collapse distance.

Kathi often works from our vacation locations. As a travel agent, she needs to visit different spas and resorts to check out their facilities. She is also given opportunities for discounts other people don't get. That's a major perk she gets for being in the travel business! While she's on the beach at the Caribbean ocean or lounging by the pool, or sitting on an outdoor terrace having lunch, she just whips out her iPad and posts writing on her blog, Blog.VacationOnYourMind.com.

Kathi posts messages once a week from wherever we are describing places she's been or companies she's worked for as an expert on travel. Every post she puts up includes her personal thoughts and photos, and the response has been fantastic. The blog was simple and inexpensive to set up on Blogspot.com initially with the help of a web master, who also did SEO that enhances the discoverability of the blog in online search engines, ensuring it gets promoted every time she blogs. When she posted pictures from Riviera Maya in Mexico that gave readers glimpses of family activities, as well as "adrenaline rush" stuff, it made people drool. The blog contains buttons that click through to a tour operation where people book their own vacations.

So, isn't it amazing how business can be conducted through the Internet no matter where you are? And more than blogging can happen. Using online communication systems, like Skype, or different applications that function on digital tablets, you can even see the people you're talking to on screen. It's the twentieth-century science fiction vision of the future come true, *Star Trek* and *2001: A Space Odyssey* wrapped up with a bow.

The following are some of the ways to use communication technology in your business.

Blogs

Like Kathi, you can blog from anywhere you are located as long as you have access to a smart phone, a tablet, or a computer. Really, smart phones are computers—just very small ones. Microchips have made emerging devices like these incredibly sophisticated.

You can set up a blog on a free system like Blogger.com, Blogspot.com, or WordPress.com. Design is easy because the systems contain user-friendly templates. You can also set up a blog on your website and have it designed in a customized way if you pay a designer to do it for you (assuming you are not skilled in Web programming yourself). The important thing is that you learn how to enter your own blog writing into the system. Blogs often include a mixture of words, images, videos, audios, and hyper-links. On the Internet, a hyperlink is a word, phrase, or image that you can click on to take you to a new document or a new section of the same document.

Blogs are a wonderful way to offer resources, training, and insights to your community. As a marketing tool, blogs are an excellent way to grow an email database of subscribers and intro-duce your business to the world.

Conference Calls/Teleseminars

When you need to get a group of any kind together on the phone for any reason and its members are located in different parts of the country or even the world, one of the easiest ways to do it is to set up a bridge line. You create an account with an Inter-net-based service like FreeConferenceCall.com or FreeConfer-ence.com, and pick a date, time, and duration on its scheduling system. The dashboards on such websites are easy to understand and operate.

After set-up, you then announce details of the call to the group by email: phone number, date, time, and password. Everyone in the group dials in from their own location at the appointed hour. You moderate the call from the online dashboard, setting up protocols like whether people are muted (lecture mode) or able to be heard (conversation mode). Choose the options from the system that make sense for your call's purpose. You can re-cord the event for future replay.

The beauty here is that the system costs nothing except charges that individuals pay to dial into the conference line (usually none if they use a mobile phone). You can use bridge line conference calls for staff meetings, group masterminds, training sessions, client consultations, and seminars. A more advanced, paid conferencing system popular with trainers is MaestroConference.com, which gives the moderator the option to split listeners into smaller interactive groups, as well as other features that we'll cover in the next section on webinars.

You can take an MP3 recording from a teleseminar and post it on your blog, or email it to a client or student so they can listen at a future time. You could also sell the audio as a product.

In addition to bridge lines, Skype also makes it possible for people to hold group calls for free from anywhere around the world, bridging them to interact through their computers. The only additional technology needed is a digital microphone and—if you want to make it a video call—a camera eye. Most laptops and tablets today have these built right into their screens. To gain access to Skype, participants need to download the free software that runs Skype onto their personal computers. For a small per-minute charge, a Skype user can dial out of the system to link with a phone. You can record a Skype call (video and audio) for posterity.

As you can plainly see, computers and phones have become combined in recent years. Statistics show that by the end of 2011, 50 percent of Americans were carrying a smart phone (iPhone, Android, Blackberry, and so on). As a result of the video, data-streaming, and Internet capabilities of these devices, the lines between phone and computer technology are only going to be further blurred in the coming years, making all different kinds of conferencing possible.

Webinars

Much like conferences calls made possible through telephone bridge lines and computer phone systems like Skype, webinars are group events that people attend via computer. The advantage of webinars is that the online technology that bridges people also makes it possible to show a slide or Power Point presentation as the host, or leader, is speaking. Popular webinar systems include InstantTeleseminar.com and StealthSeminar.net, among others. People can choose to dial in, using the system only for sound, or they can listen in on the computer and also watch the slides that accompany the webinar play. Webinars can be recorded for future replay.

We're on the board of directors of New Beginnings, a chiropractic philosophy program based in Red Bank, New Jersey, an organization providing continuing education on the philosophy, art, and science of chiropractic as well as success strategies for a rewarding practice. Besides holding weekend events at intervals during the year, New Beginnings also offers webinars for chiropractors. Jay has been a presenter for several webinars on subjects like the mistakes most new doctors make in their practices, financial independence, and marketing chiropractic services.

A video/audio recording of a webinar can be used again for a new purpose later as a product, or offered for free on a website or blog. You can make them available only to members who have access to your private website or make them generally available. It's your call. If the video is short enough it can be posted on YouTube.com. Like teleseminars, webinars are excellent marketing tools.

Radio/Internet Radio

At its essence, publicity is free advertising that you get from a third-party source. If a journalist writes an article about you or quotes you, it is publicity. If a radio or television show puts you on the air or talks about you on the air, it is publicity. If someone other than you blogs about you or your business, it is publicity. Those are all great avenues of promotion, but perhaps the easiest publicity to get is radio publicity because there are so many hours of airtime to fill on so many stations. All you need to do is pitch yourself to producers as a guest expert. When they like the pitch and think you are a fit for their program, they book you for a time slot.

Learning how to publicize your business is like learning how to do anything else. You either have to study the mechanics of it, like writing press releases, and do it yourself or you need to hire a professional. Publicists can be expensive and results can be intermittent. If you want to try making some outreaches on your own to get a sense of how it works, especially when you have something timely and newsworthy going on, like the launch of a new product or a special event taking place in the near future, you can post a press release on PRWeb.com or similar websites. They can be posted for free or for a fee that gives your release premium exposure.

Another way to reach radio producers is to purchase a directory of programs that target the same specific audience or category of information that your business does. Search the phrase "Media Directories and Databases" online and several choices will come up.

In years past, to broadcast on the radio you had to go down to the radio studio and literally sit across from the host in a sound booth. The beauty of radio production in our era is that as long as you have access to a telephone your voice can be broadcast live from anywhere. You could be on a mountaintop in Peru and, as long as you had a cell phone signal, you could go on the air.

Many people now host their own radio shows on free Internet sites like BlogTalkRadio.com. You can set an account up there if you want to host your own. These function through similar technology as webinars do. Another choice is to be a talk show host on a privately run Internet radio station that has a higher standard of production; in this way reaching a specifically targeted audience and placing yourself in the company of a group of higher quality show hosts, who could possibly help you attract attention to your own program.

Or you can go on these Internet radio station websites and study the programs they offer to see if you'd like to pitch yourself as a guest to their producers or hosts.

Social Networks

Our son Josh coordinates The New York Chiropractic Life Center's social media communication. The power of a social network like Facebook or Twitter is that it keeps you in touch with your clients on a regular basis. Create a profile in the network of your choice and let your clients know it exists. Marketing today is about forming relationships and having ongoing engagement with customers and clients. Like blogging, you can access social networks through your smart phone, tablet, or computer. Poll your customers and ask them which networks they use. You want to be where they are, communicating with them in the ways they prefer.

Permission marketing is where your customers and potential customers give you permission to communicate with them. Even if you post something every day, they find being messaged on a network less invasive and obnoxious than receiving frequent emails. In fact, they like it.

Distance Counseling and Consulting

Friends of ours who are management consultants, therapists, and workshop leaders live all over the world and run their businesses from wherever they are at the moment. The services they offer, such as counseling and consulting, are delivered one-on-one over the phone. But sometimes they lead group courses. One friend teaches four six-week-long courses every year in the form of webinars, and he's had as many as 300 students enroll. He travels and makes paid speeches, too. And for a premium hourly price, he does individual coaching. But the majority of his income now comes from teaching the group courses.

The difference between the return on your investment of twenty minutes spent with one person or spent with ten people can be significant. If you want to leverage your time, consider how you can sell your services to more than one individual simultaneously. Distance courses can include combinations of materials that deliver information to participants. You can give students a manual, a series of live webinars, recordings of the webinars, and private sessions. You could even combine an in-person experience with the rest of the mix in your program: Have everyone fly in for a weekend retreat or a week-long intensive.

Payments for individual sessions and for group sessions can be handled through an online automated shopping cart, like PayPal.com, AWeber.com, InfusionSoft.com, or 1ShoppingCart.com, or by means of a merchant account issued through a bank or a credit card company. The main rule of thumb in pricing different types of session and programs is that the closer contact a customer has with you, the higher the price goes. People expect to pay premiums for private and in-person experiences.

As you develop your Retire in Practice lifestyle, chances are good that you'll be taking advantage more often of distance-collapsing technology to stay in touch with your office staff and your customers/clients, while finding ways to boost your earnings in your work hours.

Reflection Question

Is there a service you currently offer in person that could be as effectively delivered from a remote location via phone or computer? *Hmmm.* This is food for thought.

CHAPTER 7
MAKING YOUR PLAY PAY

"It is a happy talent to know how to play."
—RALPH WALDO EMERSON

Throughout this book we've investigated different ways to leverage your time and energy to earn more with the least effort, in the process improving the quality of your life and relationships. As you've learned, with the help of modern phones and computers, location is irrelevant to certain aspects of doing business. You could be sitting on a beach on a tropical island coaching a client for an hour by telephone or leading a teleseminar for hundreds of registered listeners—or blogging, responding to emails, or planning ahead. While you're away from your office, your products can be selling off of your website, purchased through an automated shopping cart, and generating passive income for you. Your staff can be working as usual.

What more could you ask for?

Making your play pay, that's what!

Do you remember the story we told you in the Introduction about our first ski trip to Utah with our friend the dentist? He ultimately convinced us to join his group on that vacation by using the magic words, "The majority of the trip can be written off as a business expense." Being able to look forward to tax deductions is a powerful benefit of combining work with play. Since we first embraced this concept, we have created all kinds of travel opportunities for our family and friends.

The idea is simple: Build a recreational trip or sightseeing vacation around an educational program and invite a group of people you like spending time with to come—a retiring in practice strategy that helps you to generate income while you're relaxing. If you've got all the systems in place that we've described thus far, your hours are already worth three or four times a normal work hour. In addition, you can now get paid for the hours of the vacation—whether you're playing or leading a seminar. For entrepreneurially minded people, trips are ideal.

We were in our early thirties when our next door neighbor said, "I am going skiing. Come with us." He said, "Listen, it's a great trip. If you don't like skiing, you can go into Salt Lake City and have a look around. You don't have to buy any equipment, as my wife and I have stuff you can borrow. The best part is that it's a write-off because we're holding a medical-dental conference out there. We do a seminar from six to eight o'clock over breakfast, and afterwards we're on the slopes." After doing a three-day junket like this twice with our neighbors, we thought, "Why are we listening to dentists and orthopedists talking about tooth implants and hip replacements? Let's plan our own trip for chiropractors."

Twenty years ago, when we had that bright idea to put together a professional adventure to Snowbird, Utah, we decided that the theme of our seminars would be financial independence. We sent out a mailing to a large number of chiropractors we knew from the various associations we were

> *"It takes sixty-five muscles to frown and thirteen to smile. Why work overtime?"*
> —B. J. PALMER, D.C.

members of, saying that anyone interested in learning about this topic was welcome. In the end, the trip was populated by more than a dozen chiropractors and their family members, a massage therapist, a Reiki practitioner, a mortgage broker, and an accountant. With only one exception, all these individuals were self-employed.

We flew out to Utah on a Wednesday night and flew home Sunday morning. In between, we enjoyed the best skiing in the world on Thursday, Friday, and Saturday. The slopes opened at 9 A.M. During the day we would ski. At 4 P.M. we'd meet in the hot tub. Then we'd go to dinner. From 8 to 11 P.M. we held our financial independence seminar. We did that same trip five years in a row and still have the people who came asking us if we'll ever do it again!

We liked traveling so much that years ago Kathi became a travel agent. After a while the travel agent we used offered to teach her the business since she was at the agency so frequently making arrangements. In the end, it was a great decision because in this capacity, Kathi could earn commission for booking reservations for seminar participants and also write off our trips even when no meeting was planned. Part of her job requires her to look at the resorts she recommends to her customers. As a travel agent, she gets fantastic deals on accommodations, tours and attractions. But her original motivation was simply that she would book trips for our groups and secure a discount for everyone involved.

There are all kinds of financial advantages to group travel programs, not the least of which is that if you have a group over a certain size—for instance, booking ten guest-rooms—then a hotel might provide you with a meeting room for free, one free guest room, upgrades, and so on. This means you don't have to charge a lot for your programs. It's an excuse to get away and have some fun with your favorite likeminded people and, being the organizer, you can assure that your own travel expenses are covered.

There are many kinds of opportunities to make your play pay, including:

- Giving lectures at schools.
- Giving lectures on cruises.
- Holding private workshops and retreats.
- Leading tours through foreign countries.
- Attending conferences.
- Making guest appearances.
- Consulting to other business owners.

Today, we're always on the lookout for work-play opportunities. Even if we don't organize a program, Jay often gets invited to contribute to programs, for which he is given an honorarium. Being paid to show up and give a lecture or workshop is great, of course, if you can wrangle an invitation. But remember that the main thing here to focus on is the component of play. The trip must be the focus around which everything else is organized.

If you're attending a conference and your flights are already paid for, extend the trip for fun: Stay an extra day or two in the same vicinity and enjoy what the locale has to offer. Or do the opposite, take a vacation and then write off the flight by staying on a day or two to meet with clients.

Simple Trip Planning

Take your calendar of downtime and, wherever feasible, insert an event into it. Plan a trip around doing what you want to do—something you'll do whether or not someone else shows up. This trip is about taking time off from working. Its main purpose is leisure. If you get paid, too, that's like having gravy on your mashed potatoes. Remember, the priority is taking the trip.

The second step is bringing people along. (The third step is to make it profitable!) On your first trip, another couple or some friends might join you. Then, as you do trips on a regular basis those same people are likely to come again and you'll also add a few more members to your travel groups. If you can hit a baseline of required guest-rooms, hotel discounts begin to kick in that make things more affordable.

Many people try to produce enormous events without taking the time to build a reputation and community of support. In the beginning, it's not about the number of participants. It's about the quality of your program. If you shoot too high and miss your goal number, it's awkward for the participants who do sign up. To avoid this, let the participants know that it's going to be an intimate program with a lot of personal attention. Then you can grow from there. There's nothing more powerful than good word of mouth to get you ready for a more incredible second program! There might be ten people in the room with you for your first program. Let this be okay. Trust that those people will spread that positive word of mouth about what you are offering if they have fun and find your information valuable. Next time you could have 235 people in the room. Shoot for enjoying your time.

The same advice is true for building up a private practice or other business. The first five years you have to work your butt off. It's best to set reasonable goals like seeing one more patient today than yesterday, or bringing in two more clients this week than you did last week. Dial back your ego and embrace the fact that building a business takes time. Most businesses fail in the first five years of being open because their owners are not willing to go through the necessary growth phase. You have to pay your dues.

> "Everything comes to him who hustles while he waits."
> —Thomas Edison

An important concept is to start small—just put your foot on the gas pedal and go in the right direction. Thirty years later, your practice or business will be self-sustaining if your customers have been satisfied, as they'll send you new business.

Aim to be around the people you want to be around on your trip or at your event. On our trips these aren't strangers; they're friends and acquaintances. Occasionally we meet a new person who comes or a couple we know brings along another couple they know. Our friends open up new worlds to us. As our social networks expand, we also develop exciting new interests.

We don't only go on ski trips. Since 2009, we've led Retire in Practice vacation programs twice a year at resorts by the ocean in Mexico. Each time we go the trip books solidly. The itinerary includes daily workshops, volleyball games, swimming and snorkeling, visits to Mayan ruins, fine dining, and dancing. These

---

CONSIDERATIONS AND EXPENSES WHEN PLANNING A GROUP TRIP

Plan your trip yourself or contact a travel agent and delegate the planning to her. When your time is valuable, an agent can accomplish a lot more in a much shorter time and often at a much better price. It's about valuing your time and appreciating the travel agent's expertise. Expenses and logistics to determine include:

- Transportation.
- Visas, tariffs, and exit taxes.
- Accommodations.
- Meals.
- Meeting rooms.
- Guides and local tour operators.

programs are a blast—and easy to arrange!

Plan Ahead to Save Money

The best way to save money on a vacation is to go slightly off season. At many ski resorts, up through the first week in December is considered "pre-season." The price difference for a hotel room can be as much as 25–50 percent less a week prior to a peak season. This is also true of airline fares. Prices depend on more than one factor. Costs go up depending on the hotel and the season. If you take a group on a cruise, you must plan it at least six to nine months ahead to get the best prices. As categories of accommodations start disappearing, prices rise. Early on you have more choices.

In the Caribbean, the months of August and September are hurricane season, so many accommodations there are 35 to 40 percent cheaper during that time. You can't control the weather, but even if a hurricane does come through, it generally blows through in a day or two. We regularly travel to the Caribbean in the summer months and have always had great weather.

Flexibility is the key to always having a fantastic vacation. Cruises will re-route around storms if they can, rather than cancel voyages. For instance, on one cruise that a friend was on, the final destination was Fort Lauderdale. To circumvent a bad storm, the ship was rerouted to Tampa where buses were provided to bring guests back to Fort Lauderdale.

Sometimes you're in a hotel and due to bad weather (either there or at home) you are forced to extend your stay. Because you're stuck you must pay for more nights. You can switch hotels, but you are stuck in the same general location. We couldn't leave the Dominican Republic once because there was a snowstorm in New York. This had nothing to do with the weather where we were; it was just a side effect of a winter storm in the

Northeast. We had the choice of being upset or enjoying two more beautiful days until our rescheduled flight. We chose to enjoy the bonus days that the universe set up for us!

Another time we vacationed in Punta Cana (located on the eastern tip of the Dominican Republic). At the time, there were monstrous rainstorms with mudslides in the western side of the country. We had blue skies.

We've done wine tours in Napa and Sonoma in California and in the Finger Lake region of New York, which were ridiculously inexpensive since Kathi is a travel agent. Each time we brought along seven or eight friends and passed savings along to them. When Jay was invited to speak at a chiropractic conference in Peru, we created a week of incredible sightseeing prior to the conference, which added additional inspiration to Jay's presentation! We've gone out west and stayed an extra week, planning a vacation on the back of a business trip.

A big issue for you as an organizer of a travel event is to make sure you aren't laying out money up front for the trip before you've received it from participants. You can work out the details with the resort or cruise line in regard to specifications on payment. Deposits and final payments vary depending on many variables so be sure to get specifics from your travel agent.

Kathi will shop around to get the best prices available. Planning a trip in January for the following July, the first quote Kathi got included the price of meeting rooms. It seemed expensive. We decided we could have our group meet informally in the hotel library. When we took the meeting room out of the mix, the price changed significantly for the better. Be specific when you request prices.

Mileage Points and Travel Cards

Check for the best travel reward cards. Just go online and do a little research. Credit card companies are always changing and adding features. Look for the one that gives you the best mileage rewards while filling your needs. At the time of writing this book, we found that American Express had the best travel reward programs for our needs. Points add up if you pick one credit card and use it as much as possible for every purchase you charge. You don't want to go into debt, so be sure to pay down your balance in full each and every month. Then spend the points you earn on travel.

Fly with the same airlines as often as possible and enroll in their frequent flyer programs. You can rack up more mileage points that way. Basically go for the best prices and times.

If you wind up doing a lot of traveling, you'll also want to be able to get into airport clubs. The American Express Platinum card can get you into some clubs. Or you can opt for using an airline priority card instead. In an airline club you can rest during layovers or after going through security, conduct meetings, eat appetizers, drink beverages, and surf the Internet. Some clubs even have showers and changing rooms. This way you can do anything you want to make the most of your time at the airport.

We were once stuck in Minnesota from a flight cancellation due to bad weather. The airline offered to put us up in a fleabag hotel, and the helpful concierge of the airline club changed the hotel for us. She found a better place for us—and it was still paid for by the airline.

As you can see, there are many ways to support a travel habit. Don't wait until you're elderly to start traveling, retire in practice and enjoy taking trips while you're thirty, forty, fifty, sixty, and above.

Reflection Questions

Ask and answer the following questions.
- Where have you always longed to travel? (Make a list.)
- Do you favor warm weather activities or cold weather activities?
- What are your interests and hobbies? Could these be pursued during a trip? Could they be translated into a seminar or program?
- If you were going to go on vacation with six people, who would you bring?
- Do you have any business trips coming up that you could extend for a day or two of play?
- Do any of your clients live near a place you would enjoy vacationing?
- If you were going to lead a seminar, workshop, or retreat what would be your topic?
- Have you explored online travel sites or contacted a travel agency for brochures?
- Are you enrolled in points programs linked to your credit cards? (Join now.)
- Are you enrolled in one or more frequent flyer programs? (Join now.)

CHAPTER 8
BECOMING MORE ATTRACTIVE

"When you set yourself on fire, people love to come and see you burn."
—JOHN WESLEY

How do you become more attractive to the things you want to manifest in your life? You've got to set yourself on fire with a purpose that burns so brightly that you become a beacon for the universe to find you. The more passionate and excited you feel about anything you're doing, the more attractive you become. The more committed and dedicated you are, the more attractive you become. The more giving, loving, and serving you are, the more attractive you become. Then you'll bring in the right clients, patients and customers, great employees, the ideal partners to work with, and more wealth, abundance, and rewarding relationships. People love to be around positive people. If you have positive energy you'll attract everyone you need.

Manifestation of results is the same as the attraction of people on an energetic level. We believe the same universal laws and principles govern attraction as well as manifestation: Like attracts like.

Spiritual energy, which is very uplifting and resourceful, is the most powerful manifesting energy there is. By "spiritual energy," we mean the unseen forces of God, nature, Spirit, and the universe. No matter which name you personally use to refer to it, understand that when you tap into this particular energy, you tap into a quantum field of unlimited possibilities. When you do, you can consciously direct the manifestation of particular possibilities. Moreover, there is no escaping this law. The quantum field is bound by these universal laws, whether we believe in them or not, and whether they are visible to us or not. Our lives are ultimately bound by them. Spiritual energy responds to our every thought, positive or negative, conscious or unconscious. This doesn't only happen for one of us, but for all of us.

The problem here is that most of us put more emphasis on managing our physical, mental, and emotional energy than we do on managing our spiritual energy. When we ignore it we're missing the opportunity to direct its flow. But happily, it isn't hard to learn how to manage it.

This chapter will be a little different from the previous ones, but it's the most important chapter. It's the thread that flows through all the other chapters, binding them together, creating, effortlessly and synergistically, the tapestry of our lives that are before us. The more skilled we become in weaving this thread, the more magnificent the life we manifest is.

An Inside-Out Process

Becoming more attractive is an inside-out process because the flow of spiritual energy is directed by the thoughts and words we choose moment by moment. Napoleon Hill discovered this principle as he was conducting the primary research for his 1937 book *Think and Grow Rich*. Each of the massively successful businessmen he interviewed gave him the same advice: You can achieve anything that you conceive of, and believe is possible. In pragmatic terms, this means you'll attract more of what you want—everything from relationships, to success, joy abundance, wealth, and health—if you take responsibility for your thoughts and words, and strengthen the quality of your beliefs about whatever it is that you're doing. Your positive beliefs must become the truths you live your life by in order to get positive results.

Modern brain science has confirmed Hill's anecdotal evidence. The neurobiology of holding a thought, a vision, or an idea in your head for an extended period of time causes new connections and brain pathways to form that support your persistent thoughts and drive you to fulfill them. In addition, when you add the element of emotion to a mental picture, your brain believes in its reality. You can therefore "fool" yourself into living in the reality of a certain outcome before it is "real." When you find a compelling enough reason that fully engages all your senses (seeing, hearing, feeling, and, to a lesser extent, smelling and tasting), and you care about what you're doing and the people you're serving, your emotional investment will produce seemingly magical results.

Your thoughts create your reality. Your reality creates your world. So if you master your thoughts you will be in control of your destiny.

The initial three essential secrets of becoming more attractive are:

- Intention.
- Focus.
- Passion.

Those three secrets are only brought to life when the fourth secret is initiated. That fourth secret is taking inspired action. As Janet Attwood, coauthor of *The Passion Test* (Hudson Street Press, 2006), says, once you're focused on fulfilling an inspiring purpose, you must take action—and lots of it. "Strike like lightning in all directions," she advises.

There is a difference between intention and focus. Focus is physical, whereas intention is emotional. You can focus a laser beam on the wall, and you can also turn up its brightness and intensity. Intention heightens your level of focus because there is a reason behind it, such as: "Our goal is to ensure that every man, woman, and child has the opportunity to receive chiropractic care in order to ensure a healthier, more harmonious world." That intention lights your inner fire. Focus then shifts to coming up with good ideas for how to accomplish that intention, such as: talk around the world, write a book, and so on. Action is where intention is manifested.

The purpose that ultimately inspires your passion could be a project you can accomplish in the short term, or a massive vision that requires a full lifetime or more to be realized. The critical point here is using your emotion to fuel and activate your intention, motivating you to take action.

The Power of Intention

Our daughter Morgan is a great intentional manifestor. Three things proved this to us when we were on a family trip to Tobago a couple of years ago, taking a walk on a deserted beach. Every time she decided she wanted something, she created it—all within a three-hour span of time.

It was a sunny day and hot. The beach was beautiful and practically deserted. Morgan turned to us and said, "The only thing we're missing is a coconut!" We were looking at the trees. No coconuts. A minute later, an islander walked out of the jungle with a coconut he'd cut open and offered it to us. We had to pay him five bucks, but nonetheless, there it was: fresh coconut.

Next, we were swimming in the ocean. The water was so crystal clear that you could see fifteen feet down from the top. Our bodies were dangling in the waves. We were having a delightful and refreshing swim, but there were no fish. Morgan says, "The water is so clear. I wish we would see some fish." A minute or two later a giant school of fish start jumping out of the water fifty yards from where we were. There must have been 500 of them jumping out of the water and swimming around us suddenly. We thought that was cool . . . until we realized that when so many fish are swimming fast and jumping out of the water, there's usually something much bigger chasing them. We decided to leave the water and watch the show from the shore!

The last manifestation came when were strolling along the beach, looking for shells. Normally when we travel we go to all-inclusive resorts that have lots of activities; places with wind-surfing and volleyball. This was not one of those places. Morgan said, "This beach is so quiet. We really need some action." Not two minutes later, twelve armed men wearing bulletproof jackets and carrying machine guns came running out of the jungle, and they go running right past us down the beach. We were momentarily alarmed and thought we were in danger, but we relaxed as soon as we learned there had been a robbery of a motorboat. The gunmen were chasing after the thieves.

As you can see, manifesting works. But it pays to be specific about what you want. If you want action, talk about taking a boat ride. If you want fish, talk about calm, beautiful fish. If you want fresh coconut, talk about it being free so you don't have to pay for it. Be specific.

By the time Morgan started her chiropractic career, she'd already learned the lesson of specificity. She was clear that she wanted a family practice and set out to manifest it. Jay

> *"You are a living magnet. What you attract into your life is in harmony with your dominant thoughts."*
> —Brian Tracy

has never seen a lot of kids among his patients, nor had our son Josh when he partnered with Jay, even though the office had a reputation of being the family practice on the Upper West Side. But Morgan successfully manifested what she wanted. Seventy percent of her own clientele is composed of pregnant women and babies.

When saying, "I want a million bucks," say that you want to receive it in harmony with the universe. There's always a danger in being too specific in how you want to receive back from the universe. A great example of this is a story about our son, Ryan. When Ryan was four years old, all he wanted for his birthday was one hundred dollars. We thought what a cool idea it would be to put a one hundred-dollar bill in a big box for him to unwrap; we couldn't wait to see his expression when he opened his gift. To our surprise, he was extremely disappointed. We asked him what was wrong. "Isn't this what you wanted?"

He answered, "No. I want one hundred dollars." So we took back the hundred-dollar bill and gave him five twenty-dollar bills. That didn't do that trick either. Luckily for him, we ultimately realized that what he was looking for was one hundred one-dollar bills. In Ryan's case, he got what he wanted, but it took much longer than it had to because he was more concerned with the form in which his request was manifested than in the fact that the universe had complied with his wish. The lesson? Don't impede the universe's ability to give to you. Just trust that it will.

Before we go on, we want to clarify the ideas of "positive" and "negative." It's important to appreciate that there is no positive or negative. They are judgments.

Have you ever heard the expression "One man's junk is another man's gold?" We read a true story once about a man who volunteered to help a local zoo by carting off the tons of elephant poop that was produced on a weekly basis. It might have been crap for the zoo, but this gentleman felt he'd struck gold. He was a modern-day alchemist who turned elephant poop into "gold." Well, not really gold, but fertilizer that he sold for a very high premium.

So our question is, was it poop or was it gold? Was this poop bad or good? In the famed words of Yogi Berra, "It ain't nothing 'til I call it!"

Our advice is to reserve your judgments and figure out how to use the poo life gives you as fertilizer to grow your dreams. Throughout this chapter, rather than using the typical phrases, like positive belief, negative belief, positive outcome, and negative outcome, we will be using the terms "resourceful" and "unresourceful." The difference is that resourceful things bring you closer to your desired outcomes and unresourceful things will often not give you the outcome you desire. When we do use the words "positive" and "negative," they are not meant as judgments but as directions for things moving you forward or holding you back.

Be careful to avoid harboring unresourceful beliefs. People often manifest things they don't want because that is what they focus on. Most people spend more time contemplating and focusing on what they don't want rather than on directing their energy toward focusing and concentrating on what they do want.

One of the universal laws is that you always get what you focus on. A friend's father was diagnosed with cancer. When the doctor told him he had three months to live this man bought into it fully. Three months to the day, he died. His belief in his diagnosis was so strong that his brain rewired to match his new truth, and he fulfilled his outcome to the day.

A little over a year later, our friend's mother was given a similar diagnosis, but her belief was that the body can heal anything, and so she directed her energy towards the healing process and away from the disease process. By doing this, her life expectancy far exceeded the death sentence of the diagnosis. She lived a mostly healthy, almost symptom-free life for years.

Same diagnosis, same cancer, different belief system.

Resourceful beliefs with positive actions show up as a positive manifestation pattern. For instance, both of us trust the manifestation process to such an extent that we take full responsibility for everything that happens in our lives, knowing that we have complete control to change our outcomes by changing our thoughts and focus. One of our credos is: If you don't like the results you're getting, change what you're doing (thoughts, focus, and action)!

By always taking one hundred percent credit for your outcomes, you own the power to change them. In that instant, you take control of your destiny and can no longer play the role of a victim of circumstance.

Unresourceful beliefs show up as a negative manifestation pattern. For instance, no matter where the ex-boyfriend of our friend Stephanie went, he always met someone who picked a fight with him. He caused it. Even if he was sitting still doing nothing, he manifested hostile responses. She told us she had to break up with him because she couldn't stand being around so much conflict. The important thing to understand is that, for the most part, it was an unconscious energy on his part.

To safeguard yourself against problem manifestations like this one, avoid saying things like:

- "How much more of this am I going to get?"
- "Whenever I go on vacation I get sick."
- "People always bump into me on the street."

The most powerful two-word question that will always perpetuate the reasons you get what you don't want is: "Why me?" The reason these two words hold so much power is due to the nature of the brain. Like a search engine on the Internet, when posed with a question, the brain will search for an infinite number of answers to justify the question. Your brain doesn't differentiate between good or bad, right or wrong, positive or negative results. Its only concern is to answer the question with no pre-conceived judgment filters.

Remember, if you declare it, to the universe that is the same as asking for it.

Another useful guideline is to be mindful of the company you keep. You'll become most like the people with whom you associate most often. Who do you hang out with? Are you hanging out with the "I cans" or the "I can'ts," the "everything is possible" people or the "everything is impossible" people? We think it's important to keep company with uplifting, positive people.

Look at the seven people you associate with the most (family, friends, coworkers, and so on). Ask yourself whether they support you in the dreams and outcomes that you have or tend to hold you back? You will become most like the books you read, the shows you watch, the teachers you listen to, and the people you associate with. Therefore our suggestion is to choose wisely...very, very wisely.

Reframing Unresourceful Beliefs

If you have an unresourceful belief system, how can you replace those beliefs with resourceful beliefs that will manifest better results for you? First you have to be aware that an unresourceful belief exists and may be holding you back. We know that may sound silly, but an important first step is to monitor your thought processes. Lots of people live with unresourceful beliefs and don't realize it.

Others know their unresourceful beliefs are there, but think they can't be changed. Beliefs can be shifted by new choices coupled with action.

If you want to change a belief, the first thing to do is to acknowledge it. Then ask yourself resourceful questions about it. Resourceful thinking leads to solutions. Unresourceful thinking reinforces problems. Resourcefulness adds to your quality of life. Unresourcefulness detracts from your quality of life. You may want to ask yourself,

- "What do I need to do different?"
- "Who do I need to consult?"
- "Where do I need to go for more information?"
- "When do I need to take action"
- "How can I improve on this outcome?"

Never ask "why" questions. Why questions only serve to discover more why questions! They are great for research, but not very strong in generating powerful outcomes.

No thought by itself is positive or negative, resourceful or unresourceful. They carry no weight until you place a judgment on them."Bad" and "good" depend upon the context. Thoughts are only "bad" if you would prefer a different outcome than the one they lead to. Let's say you are overweight and would like to slim down. A resourceful question would be: "How can I reduce my food intake and feel better about myself?"

An unresourceful question would be: "Why am I so fat?" The second question doesn't give you insight into an alternative behavior you could try. It merely reinforces mentally what you are already doing. It is unresourceful because it just gives you all the reasons you are so fat!

Underneath all behaviors lie rewards, benefits that motivate us—even if we're not aware of them. Someone who is grossly overweight may know it's not healthy, know it's affecting his or her lifestyle, and know he or she should change. But being heavy may mean to him or her that he or she doesn't "have to" do things to impress people or that he or she doesn't have to exercise. Those are beliefs.

Such a person may have a secondary gain, such as: "If I stay this weight I don't have to change my life" or "I don't have to go hiking with everyone else." It allows this person to stay in his or her comfort zone without the risk of feeling guilty.

Asking "How does this belief serve me?" is a highly resourceful question, because it will generate the feedback you need to help you understand what's motivating you on a subconscious level. This leads you to making more resourceful choices, manifesting more of what you want. When you want to change your results, you need to change your thoughts that will change your behaviors, and, when these changes are maintained long enough, they will change your beliefs, completing the cycle of manifesting a more resourceful outcome.

The old adage "When at first you don't succeed, try, try again" addresses the need for persistence in achieving a goal. However, we like to think of it as: "When at first you don't succeed, try something different." This addresses the fact that you do something different to improve the chances of achieving your desired outcome. Albert Einstein's definition of insanity is doing the same over and over again (try, try again without changing what you do) and expecting different results. To demonstrate and reinforce your sanity, be persistent in your direction and be flexible in your method of getting there!

One of the best examples of persistence with flexibility without losing sight of your goal is our son Ryan. He always knew what he wanted and was able to figure out how to use the word "no" as a signal not to stop or give up, but to do something different to achieve his desired outcome. When he was very young, he asked if he could have a Coke. We said no, but in Ryan's mind, that was the signal to engage his creativity and do something different. He proceeded to ask for a cola, a soda, a Pepsi, a soft drink. He continued until we finally succumbed to his persistence. We learned a lesson in the importance of being flexible in getting what you want!

Many businesspeople experience an unsettling feeling of fear when they are growing their businesses. They feel fearful of change, of the unknown, of making a mistake, of appearing foolish, of what others may think and say about them, and of losing control of their lives if they succeed. Sometimes even when people know that doing something new could improve their lives, they won't do it because it means going into unknown territory. Inside they hit a wall of resistance. That's how the fear of change holds us back. It's well known that most small businesses fail within the first five years—fear is one of the reasons why.

If you knew Jay you would probably find it hard to believe that he used to be very quiet and shy. He had to force himself to talk to people. He would give adjustments in his office without uttering a word. People would come in, lie down on his table, he'd adjust them, and then they'd leave and say, "Thanks, see you on Wednesday, Doc." Eventually he realized he'd do more good if he started communicating the chiropractic story to his patients and their families. The first time he stood in front of an audience he felt uncomfortable. But he decided to believe he was the "best orator in the room" and then fake it until he really was. Being more attractive is about putting what you want out into the world by being it.

The Law of Reciprocity

Throughout this book we've been discussing various things you can do to get more time, money, and energy than you have now.

We've been exploring how you can balance your career and personal life, and find the most rewarding mixture of work and play for you. We've also been discovering ways to build teams and sources of passive income that liberate you from your workplace, as well as how to use advanced technology and online systems to serve your clients, patients and customers remotely—either from home or from a vacation destination. By now the mental picture you've been developing of your Retire in Practice lifestyle must be sharper than ever. Reinforcing your vision of the life you want, in all its dimensions, is the key to its creation.

As you become clearer about your purpose—a purpose you are emotionally attached to—and develop this vision, you will become magnetic, bringing people, resources, and opportunities into your sphere of influence at the speed of light! Underlying this phenomenon is metaphysical magnetism, or the law of reciprocity: What you put out comes back to you—and in greater measure.

With our own money we've found that when we donate to a cause we strongly believe in and care about, our gift comes back to us tenfold. Not necessarily in the same way or from the source we gave it to. But it does come back. And we always get back more than we have given. Give more of yourself in a human way and also in a financial way. Many times we've been asked to donate and step up to the plate for a cause when it hasn't been easy to come up with the money. One time we donated anyway because we knew it was for a bigger cause. A week later we got stuck in a Florida airport where we ended up being given six additional free tickets by the airline to compensate us for being inconvenienced. We knew that this was the universe fulfilling the law of reciprocity. We donated $500 dollars (that we really didn't have), and received over $6,000 dollars' worth of airline tickets! Our lives have always revolved around the belief that you can never out-give the giver. The universe is limitless and infinite in all possibilities. You just have to be open, receptive, and, most importantly, grateful in order to receive.

If you want to pull the people, things, and opportunities you want toward you like a magnet, you've got to put out the qualities that you're looking for in the ways you think, believe, feel, speak, and act. What you put out you get back. That's the law of reciprocity working on your behalf, bringing you objects and experiences that represent or match those qualities. Reciprocity is at play in every area of your life from business to relationships, money, and health. If you want more love, love more. If you want to feel more appreciated, appreciate those around you. If you want more abundance in your life, give freely from your heart.

Years ago an Italian man arrived in New York City without a penny in his pocket. He somehow scraped up enough to buy a hotdog cart and over the years became successful as a street vendor. At lunchtime there was always a line of people waiting at his cart to buy his hotdogs because he always had the best rolls, he always gave his customers the biggest hotdogs he had and two scoops of sauerkraut, and he always smiled and had something good to say. Although the man wasn't wealthy, he earned enough from operating that hotdog cart six days a week to buy a small house and put his three kids through college.

Then his eldest son graduated from college with a business degree. The boy came home and told his dad he was going to help him run his business. "We can save money and increase our profit margin if we use a smaller hotdog, Pop," he said. "It's okay. No one will know. We also don't have to buy the buns from the best bakery; we can get them from a commercial bakery. Plus, you should just put one scoop of sauerkraut on every hotdog instead of two scoops."

When he heard these ideas, the father thought, "I guess my son is smarter than I am. After all, he went to college. So I'll follow his advice." He changed his business practices and his son was right: his profits per individual hotdog skyrocketed. Unfortunately, his overall earnings went down. After several months there was no longer a line of hungry customers waiting to get his hotdogs. No one said hello to him on the street anymore. After a while, the street vendor lost his business. Where he once had reaped benefits from giving of himself to his customers, serving the people without thinking about what he was gaining, the focus of the pushcart business went from serving and exceeding the expectations of his patrons to being all about business and income. Everyone could sense the difference.

Being intentional is more important than anything else you could do to build and market your business. Intention is the inspiring reason, the why, behind doing what you do. And it is the vision of the outcome you want that leads you to become intentional. Your intention is powerful because it directs your focus to things that matter. When you focus on areas of significance, your next action steps are revealed. Intention is attention coupled with emotion. From there, it's a matter of allowing the world to respond.

We respond to the world and the world responds to us in a giant feedback loop. If something you're doing isn't working, before giving up ask, "What about this is not working?" and, more importantly "What do I need to do to make it work?" Just because it can't work in the way you're doing it doesn't mean you have to abandon your vision. The vision is still the same.

If your vision is to travel from New York to California in under a week and you begin by walking, the answer is not to walk faster; it's to find another mode of transportation. You might walk for one day and see, from the feedback you get, that you only covered twenty miles. At this point you notice, "Hmm. That was interesting. How could I get a better result?" Rather than blaming or shaming yourself, and saying, "I screwed up!" take responsibility for the results and then make a point to be innovative in the future.

For a Retire in Practice lifestyle, you need to build a practice or business that brings you enough income to give you financial and time freedom while being structured in such a way that you can take time off for leisure or volunteering. Successful businesses are not built on marketing alone. Although a tempting offer may get people through the door the first time, it ultimately takes more than this to keep people coming back. Everybody expects good service these days, so you have to go beyond it. You have to exceed people's expectations. Real magic in marketing comes from genuinely giving of yourself to the people you serve, from building relationships and loyalty. In Jay's practice, he has always believed that if he serves his members unconditionally, the money he needs will always be there, and it has been.

Having a Life Purpose and Mission

Having a life purpose means having a reason for being that's bigger than you. This reason isn't just a short-term goal or career track. Your mission should outlast you. It's the inspiring answer to the underlying lifestyle question of why you'd even want to have more time, energy, and money. It's the legacy you want to leave. It's what you want people to be saying about you at your funeral and for years after. In short, it's about what you stand for and the impact you've made on the world.

Do you know your "why"? For us, the bigger reason of what we do is making sure that every man, woman, and child has the opportunity to receive a chiropractic adjustment and a chiropractic education if they choose. Everything we do brings us closer to achieving that mission, but we know we can never finish it. It's something we can't accomplish on our own. It's that big a purpose.

When you find a life purpose that you're passionate about, this discovery leads to the development of a vision. You begin to realize how other people are going to be part of it. You begin to make a positive impact on the planet or a community. That's why the vision outlives you and not you it. Where does attraction factor in? The more focused and specific you get about your vision, the more people can see you and become enrolled in your plans.

A life purpose translates into intentions and action steps. You'll be more focused on achieving your purpose if you develop a clear vision of it. The following questions may help.

First, think of someone you know and deeply respect who is living the lifestyle you want. Holding this person in mind, what are the three top qualities you admire in him or her?

When you are at your best, who are you? What adjectives would describe your best self?

What additional skills, values, or traits would help you improve your quality of life?

Jump ahead to the end of your life. Looking backwards from the future, what would you say are the three most important lessons you've learned? Why

> "Start telling a better-feeling story about the things that are important to you. Do not write your story like a factual documentary, weighing all the pros and cons of your experience, but instead tell the uplifting, fanciful, magical story of the wonder of your own life and watch what happens. It will feel like magic as your life begins to transform right before your eyes, but it is not by magic. It is by the power of the laws of the universe and your deliberate alignment with those laws."
> —ABRAHAM-HICKS

are they so critical?

Reflect on these and similar questions until you develop a full-blown vision of a specific reality that encompasses the manifestation of your life purpose. Then step into the picture.

Visualizing Your Goals

Our friend and colleague Joe Dispenza, D.C., author of *Breaking the Habit of Being Yourself* (Hay House, 2012) is an expert on brain science and an advocate of visualization. He says we manifest whatever we think about on a subconscious level. So he recommends deciding how you want your next day to be, and playing the day out in detail right before you go to bed at night.

Ask: "What do you think went well today and how do you want tomorrow to go?"

Night time is our "big picture" time. After we get into bed, we give thanks for what we have and, before going to sleep, we take turns answering the question, "What do I want to do next?"

When you consciously intend to do something, people that support this goal are brought into your life. Recently Jay had a vision of becoming an international speaker. It seemed like the next level or stage in his life from where he had been professionally. He began holding the thought of speaking around the world and getting honorariums to do it, and we began talking about his vision for it and discussing it with a few close friends. As soon as he put it out there, we started meeting people who could make this dream come true: people from Spain, Peru, Scotland, and New Zealand. When it wasn't in our consciousness they weren't in our life.

These people didn't come out of the blue and say, "Hi Jay, I'm from here, would you come speak?" We brought the subject up when opportunities presented, for instance, meeting a Peruvian chiropractor and mentioning that Jay wanted to speak to foreign audiences. But until Jay became clear and emotionally committed to the idea that this was what he wanted to do there weren't any opportunities. Or if there were opportunities, we didn't notice them.

It took a couple of years of working on this concept for it to begin to manifest. Originally Jay was visualizing the speaking engagements, but he forgot to put in the part about being paid. He was invited to Barcelona and we had our room and board paid for, but we had to cover our own airfare. Then he made an adjustment to his vision and now payment is manifested, too. Most of Jay's speeches revolve around many of the subjects in this book, as well as success principles, communication strategies, the laws of attraction, and chiropractic philosophy.

An important element of any visualization is the incorporation of your five senses. When you set the goal, "five-sense" it by imagining what the fully realized outcome looks, feels, sounds, tastes, and smells like. Concept it in order to get the outcome you most would like. Visualize every part of it like you would if you were scripting or directing a scene from a movie. Leave nothing to chance in your visualization. As Stephen R. Covey wrote in *The 7 Habits of Highly Effective People* (Free Press, 1989), "Begin with the end in mind." This way you can rerun the same visualization over and over, and watch it come into a sharper focus, creating new brain synapses and neurology that's aligning your thoughts with your actions.

From the visualization you will discover a plan of how to get it. From the plan you will discover the action steps to take. And, as you begin to execute those steps, you'll have real-life opportunities to reassess and reinforce the plan and make course corrections. This is how visualization becomes a pragmatic and three-dimensional tool for manifestation.

The brain has a function called the reticular activating system (RAS), which is tasked with filtering out what is unimportant to you and filtering in what is important to you. So if you constantly think about seeing the same images, your brain shows them to you in the world around you. Let's say, for example, that you were looking to buy a unique car. You would look around and, failing to find a dark green Saab, decide no one has one. You'd place your order. Then, because you've brought this car into your consciousness, all of sudden everywhere you went from then on you'd be passing dark green Saabs.

It's also essential to put yourself into the picture. A friend of Jay's used to tell him how he'd sit and visualize a red Cadillac convertible he wanted for at least twenty minutes every day. That was all he thought about for those twenty minutes. One day he went to the window of his high-rise apartment and looked down into the street below. There was the exact Cadillac he had been envisioning, except that someone else was driving it! The moral of this story is that you always should make sure you are in the picture. You want to be part of the future you are visualizing.

There is a very simple test to determine how much you embody your vision. If, when you think about your vision, it appears as a still picture, or in black and white, you're not there yet. If the picture is in color, you're a little closer. When the color picture becomes a movie that you are watching, you're getting really warm. When you step into the picture and you are no longer the observer, you are now living your vision with full emotion and sensory input. It's only at this point that your visualization triggers manifestation.

> "Cherish your visions and your dreams as they are the children of your soul, the blueprints of your ultimate achievements."
> —NAPOLEON HILL

A Popular Tool for Manifestation: The Vision Board

The clearer and more five-sensed your image of the end result you want to experience is, the likelier it is to come to fruition, and because 70 percent of the world's population is visual, the majority of us benefit from visualization. One of the tools that can help you manifest results in your life is a vision board. This is where you paste images and messages on a poster board as a collage in order to reinforce the mental picture of anything you'd like to create. Boards are powerful reinforcements for intentions because the mind thinks in pictures.

The purpose behind boards is to trigger an emotional response in you every time you pass them and see those images. You think, "Wow, I'm getting closer to having that! I want that!"

Our friend Stephanie made two vision boards on New Year's Eve a couple of years ago. One was about moving and dancing and travel and all the other physical activities she likes to do. The other was about money and objects. She hung both on the wall near her front door so she'd see them when she was going in and out of her house. After the money board was on her wall for a couple of months she had the realization that she didn't want any of the stuff she'd put on it. None of it was motivating her. In time, the board helped her see those things weren't her authentic desires.

Stephanie felt differently about the other board. Every time she saw it she got excited. It raised her energy and inspired her with thoughts of traveling, dancing, and socializing with like-minded people. That board helped her be intentional about the fulfillment of her desires.

Bringing the vision board into the twenty-first century is as easy as downloading pictures and images from the web, creating backgrounds, screen savers, and slide shows for your computer and smart phone. And if you want to kick up the effectiveness of your high-tech vision board, add music and sound to it. Music and other types of sound are very powerful emotional anchors. Of course, you can also export copies of the vision board and place these printouts in strategic areas around your home and office so that your vision or dream is always in the forefront of your mind, both consciously and, more importantly, subconsciously.

We have found two websites dedicated specifically to creating vision boards. Their templates make the process super easy. Visit VisionBoardSite.com and MakeaVisionBoard.com and try it out for yourself. A book on making vision boards that we recommend is Michelle Nielsen's *Manifesting Matisse* (Book Surge, 2008), a beautiful step-by-step guide to manifesting in your life, inspired by her personal experiences.

Meditation

Another tool for manifestation we like and use every single day of our lives is mediation. Meditation is the art of quieting your educated mind and turning off the outside world long enough to be able to connect with your inner voice. In this altered state, the power of suggestion, focused visualization, and healing are fostered and integrated into every cell of your body, allowing you to create the things you want in life.

For most people, guided meditations are the easiest way to get into the state of awakened consciousness where manifestation has its roots.

We have three favorite sources for guided meditations. As soon as we wake up, we play the morning guided meditation we've set up ready to go on our iPods. We have been listening to meditations by Chuck (River) Ribley, D.C., for more than 25 years. We start our day this way to get centered and ready for the day. These are the meditations that started every morning of the Inner Winners Seminars that River, his wife, Ruth, and we poured our hearts and souls into delivering to the public for so many years! It's a testament to the timelessness of these meditations that we still like them! And in fact, these meditations (we love the centering and rainbow meditations especially) are still available for sale. Just email River at ChuckRibley@yahoo.com and let him know how you heard about them.

During the day, we will take a break and listen to a power meditation that helps us to reinforce our focus for the rest of the day. We enjoy listening to short meditations by Michelle Nielsen, D.C. These short meditations help to silence your external talk and allow you to be transported to a safe place where you can reinforce what you want in life. For more information and to order one or all of Michelle's meditations, go to her website, MasterManifestors.com.

For one of the most powerful deep trance meditations there are, use the manifestation manifestations that Dr. Joe Dispenza has created. These will help you transport your mind to a place where visualization and manifestation transform to reality, and quickly! Joe teaches about the quantum field (aka the field of unlimited possibilities), and how to tap into it to manifest whatever you want in your life! Just as we taught our children, he did the same with his and they are amazing manifestors as well! We set aside an hour of the day to do Joe's meditations. They are so powerful that after listening to one for the first time and focusing on one thing I wanted to manifest, an hour after the meditation was over I received a phone call and, just like that, my vision became reality! To order these meditations, go to DrJoeDispenza.com.

You're probably thinking, *Wow, I could never do all of these meditations every day!* Don't worry. Just do one at least once a day. On days where you are just relaxing, you can add another. On vacation?

That's the perfect time to enjoy more. Once you start, you won't want to stop!

Emotions Are the "Secret Ingredient" of Manifestation

Every chef has something he adds to his recipes that makes them special, a secret sauce or special garnish or ingredient that makes his dishes over-the-top delicious. The same is true in visualization: There's an ingredient that makes each of us feel over-the-top excited about the outcomes we're imagining and spending time focusing. That "secret ingredient" is our emotional connection to the outcome. It's whatever meaning stirs up our passion.

A vision without passion is like an oil painting: It's pretty to look at, and nice to talk about, but it's sterile. Passion brings it to life. Emotions help you believe in the reality of the vision. If there's no emotion involved in your dream then you don't believe it; it's just sitting there, lifelessly. Your passion triggers everything to come into fruition.

Napoleon Hill said we should get up each day and ask, "How can I serve more people today in what I do? How can I improve on what I am already doing to help them?" There is scientific evidence that we're hardwired for altruism and taking care of each other. Senior citizens who volunteer are healthier and experience less dementia than those who don't. When you figure out what values you resonate with, and get a handle on where these fit into your life, then you've found a stronger source of motivation than having a million bucks piling up interest in the bank.

Whenever you identify something you want to attract, ask the following four questions.

- "Does what I want to attract align with my vision?"
- "Is my focus concentrated on having what I want?"

- "Do I have a power of intention (a compelling reason) for having what I want?"
- "Have I started taking massive, immediate action to get what I want?"

Be 100 percent clear on what you want to attract. This is the simple, yet powerful secret to getting what you want in life. If you focus on the why, the how will take care of itself and you'll have an action-packed, fulfilling life.

Managing Your Fear of Change

Often people get nervous when their visualizations begin to come true. It's ironic, but true. That's because we're hardwired to resist change and the unknown. Primitive people knew that if they saw something unusual happening in the environment around them it was a sign of danger. The rustling of the tall grasses could indicate a lion readying to pounce and people couldn't take that risk. The human brain is designed to identify patterns and doesn't like it when the pattern changes. For the most part we therefore prefer to be able to predict what's going to happen.

Nowadays there are few tigers lying in wait to eat us. The things we get nervous about really aren't life threatening, though we respond to them as if they were. And we make up things to be afraid of, because the brain wants to persuade us not to change our patterns of behavior. There's a popular phrase that describes this tendency of the brain to look for evidence of danger: "FEAR is false evidence appearing real." We don't know who originally invented that saying, but it is a clever mnemonic device that we say to ourselves to not let fear stop us. As our colleague Martha Nessler

> "Genius is 1 percent inspiration and 99 percent perspiration."
> —THOMAS EDISON

says, "Fear is conquered by HOPE: helping open people's eyes."

The Seven Steps of Intentional Creation

One of the main ways to override fear is to tap into your passion. Once you have an idea in mind for a manifestation there is a very particular way to bring it to fruition. The following steps of intentional creation are designed to overcome the problem of fear. Use this seven-step process daily until your creation has occurred. Particularly, be sure to take action (step 7). Visualization without action may feel good, but it won't lead to creation!

1. On a regular basis, what thoughts do you focus on that you do not want to create in your life?
2. List five unresourceful thoughts you have.
3. List five things you would love to create in your life.
4. What are the top four obstacles preventing you from creating what you want?
5. What is holding you back from overcoming each of these obstacles?
6. For each obstacle, list one action step that you can take within the next twenty-four hours that would start eliminating it.
7. Take the action step.

> ENVISION IT.
> BELIEVE IT.
> START IT.
> DO IT . . .
> 'TIL IT'S DONE.
> AND HAVE FUN!

Recommended Resources

Dr. Jay Handt and Kathi Handt
RetireinPractice.com
Check our website for updates, free stuff, and special events. We
are available to do speaking engagements with organizations and
groups.

Inspired Teachers

Dr. Eric Plasker
100YearLifestyle.com

Dr. Joe Dispenza
DrJoeDispenza.com

Dr. Michelle Nielsen
MasterManifestors.com

Chiropractic Organizations

Life University
Life.edu

New Beginnings Chiropractic Philosophy Weekends
NBChiro.com

International Chiropractic Pediatric Association
ICPA4Kids.com

International Chiropractic Association
Chiropractic.org

Life Chiropractic College West
LifeWest.edu

League of Chiropractic Women
LCWomen.com

International Federation of Chiropractic Organizations
IFCOChiro.org

ChiroEurope
ChiroEuropeSeminar.com

Barcelona College of Chiropractic
BCChiropractic.es

New Zealand College of Chiropractic
Chiropractic.ac.nz

Mission Life International/Dr. Peter Morgan
Mission-Chiropractic.com

ChiroMission
ChiroMission.org

"The Best Mission Trip Ever"
TheBestMissionTripEver.com

Travel Programs

For mileage reward programs, go to the airlines you travel, search for their program and join. There is no fee. Just do it.

If you are a Delta Sky Miles member, go to SkyMilesShopping.com and register. You can accumulate more miles when you shop online through their portal. Miles accumulate fast!

Recommended
Reading

Janet Attwood and Chris Attwood. *The Passion Test: The Effortless Path to Discovering Your Life Purpose*. New York: Plume, 2008.

Richard Bandler and John Grinder, *Frogs into Princes: Neuro Linguistic Programming*. Lafayette, CA.: Real People Press, 1979.

Richard Bandler, *Richard Bandler's Guide to Trance-formation: How to Harness the Power of Hypnosis to Ignite Effortless and Lasting Change*. Florida: Health Communications Inc., 2008.

Richard Bandler and John Grinder, *The Structure of Magic*. Palo Alto, CA.: Science and Behavior Books, 1975.

Michael Brooks, *Instant Rapport!* New York: Grand Central Publishing, 1990.

Samuel Butler, *Erewhon*. 1872.

James L. Chestnut, M.Sc.., D.C., C.C.W.P., *The Wellness Prevention Paradigm*. Victoria, B.C., Canada: The Wellness Practice—Global Self Help Corp., 2011.

Robert B. Cialdini, *Influence: The Psychology of Persuasion*. New York: HarperBusiness, 2006.

George S. Clason, *The Richest Man in Babylon*. 1926.

Stephen R. Covey, *The Seven Habits of Highly Effective People: Powerful Lessons in Personal Change*. New York: Free Press, 2004.

Thomas Crum, *The Magic of Conflict: Turning a Life of Work into a Work of Art*. New York: Touchstone, 1998.

F.P. DeGiacomo, *Man's Greatest Gift to Man—Chiropractic*. New York: LSR Learning Associates, 1978.

Joe Dispenza, D.C., *Evolve Your Brain: The Science of Changing Your Mind*. Florida: Health Communications Inc., 2007.

Joe Dispenza, D.C., *Breaking the Habit of Being Yourself: How to Lose Your Mind and Create a New One*. Carlsbad, CA.: Hay House, 2012.

Joe Dominguez and Vicki Robin with Monique Tilford, *Your Money or Your Life: 9 Steps to Transforming Your Relationship with Money and Achieving Financial Independence: Revised and Updated for the 21st Century*. New York: Penguin, 2008.

Dianne Dukette and David Cornish, *The Essential 20: Twenty Components of an Excellent Health Care Team*. RoseDog Books, 2009.

Wayne W. Dyer, *Gifts from Eykis*. New York: HarperPaperbacks, 2002.

T. Harv Eker, *Secrets of the Millionaire Mind: Mastering the Inner Game of Wealth*. New York: HarperBusiness, 2005.Timothy Ferriss, *The 4-Hour Workweek: Escae 9-5, Live Anywhere, and Join the New Rich*. New York: Crown Archetype, 2009.

Napoleon Hill, *Think and Grow Rich*. 1937.

Kevin Hogan, *The Science of Influence: How to Get Anyone to Say "Yes" in 8 Minutes or Less.* New York: John Wiley and Sons, 2010.

Gerald C. Jampolsky, M.D., and Diane V. Cirincione, *Change Your Mind, Change Your Life*. New York: Bantam, 1994.

Jonah Lehrer, *How We Decide*. New York: Mariner Books, 2010.

Bruce H. Lipton, Ph.D., *The Biology of Belief: Unleashing the Power of Consciousness, Matter & Miracles*. Carlsbad, CA.: Hay House, 2011.

Jim Loehr and Tony Schwartz, *The Power of Full Engagement: Managing Energy, Not Time, Is the Key to High Performance and Personal Renewal*. New York: Free Press, 2004.

Michelle K. Nielsen, D.C., *Manifesting Matisse: A Practical System for Reality Creation*. Book Surge Publishing, 2008.

B.J. Palmer, *The Bigness of the Fellow Within*. Spartanburg, S.C.: Sherman College of Straight Chiropractic, 1978.

Daniel H. Pink, *Drive: The Surprising Truth about What Motivates Us*. New York: Riverhead Trade, 2011.

Eric Plasker, D.C., *The 100 Year Lifestyle: Dr. Plasker's Breakthrough Solution for Living Your Best Life—Every Day of Your Life!* Avon, MA.: Adams Media, 2007.

Guy F. Riekeman, D.C., *Make Your Life Extraordinary.* Georgia: Life University Press, 2007.

Anthony Robbins, *Awaken the Giant Within: How to Take Immediate Control of Your Mental, Emotional, Physical and Financial Destiny!* New York: Free Press, 1992.

Anthony Robbins, *Unlimited Power: The New Science of Personal Achievement.* New York: Free Press, 1997.

Patricia Schultz, *1,000 Places to See Before You Die.* New York: Workman, 2011.

Ralph Stephensen, D.C., *The Chiropractic Textbook.* 1927.

Stuart Wilde, *The Trick to Money Is Having Some.* Carlsbad, CA.: Hay House, 1995.

Norman Vincent Peale, *The Power of Positive Thinking,* New York: Prentice-Hall, 1952.

ABOUT THE AUTHORS

JAY HANDT, D.C., and KATHI HANDT are a husband and wife creative team.

Ranked as one of the Top 10 Chiropractors in New York for 2006 and 2007 by the Consumer Research Council of America's Guide to America's Top Chiropractors, Dr. Jay Handt founded The New York Chiropractic Life Center in 1978 on the Upper West Side of Manhattan. He is a graduate of York College (The City University of New York) and The New York Chiropractic College, a diplomate of the National Board of Chiropractic Examiners, a member of the Board of Trustees of Life University, where he is also a President's Circle member and is on the board of directors of New Beginnings Seminars. He teaches on the post-graduate faculty of Life University, as well as at Palmer College of Chiropractic and Sherman College of Straight Chiropractic. He is a founding member of The New York Chiropractic Council, and a member of the International Chiropractic Pediatric Association and the Florida Chiropractic Society.

Jay lectures on chiropractic care, personal growth, and motivation nationwide, and creates programs for groups and businesses, depending on their needs. He presents ropes courses to prospective students at Life University, allowing the participants to develop and focus on skills for achieving personal growth in all phases of life. For more than twenty years, Jay has also presented fire walking programs to help people break free from their limitations.

Kathi Handt holds a bachelor's degree and a master's degree in music from Brooklyn College, and her creativity is evident in everything she does. She has been a personal growth seminar leader, a motivational speaker, and a certified ropes course facilitator. She is on the board of directors of New Beginnings Seminars. In partnership with Jay, and with Ruth and Dr. Chuck Ribley, Kathi taught and facilitated at the Inner Winners Seminars, a program that guided participants to move through limiting beliefs to reach their full potential. She currently lectures on leadership and teamwork for chiropractic students considering enrollment at Life University.

Kathi works closely with Jay on all of his programs, from creation to implementation. She is now in the research stages of finding ways to bring chiropractic to those in need all over the world, and has a special place in her heart for the children of the world. Kathi is also one of the founders and organizers of Business Success Team, a networking group whose purpose is for its members to support each other with sound business tips and referrals. She is also a founding member and executive board member of League of Chiropractic Women, an organization bringing women to the forefront in chiropractic leadership, politics and success, and speaks internationally. In addition to raising three children, she has worked as a stock and bond broker, real estate broker, and travel agent.

Kathi and Jay are active in community service. Together they have donated their time and talents to ChiroMission and Chiromissions, organizations that deliver free chiropractic care to thousands in the Dominican Republic, Haiti, Trinidad, and Cuba, to the Marine Corps' "Toys for Tots" program to help the needy, and to City Harvest food drives. It is their mission to help others constantly create excellence in their health and lives.

Visit the Handts online at RetireInPractice.com.

ABOUT THE CO-WRITER

STEPHANIE GUNNING is the co-writer or ghostwriter of over twenty-five books, including *Audacious Creativity*, *Total Renewal*, *Easy Homeopathy*, *Exploring Feng Shui*, *The American Institute of Homeopathy Handbook for Parents*, *The Passion Principle*, *You Are a Spirit*, *Whiff*, and *The Sedona Method*. As an editor and publishing consultant, her clients have included bestselling authors, like Gregg Braden and Hale Dwoskin, major publishing firms, top-caliber literary agencies, and innovative self-publishers.

Stephanie's career began at HarperCollins Publishers and Bantam Doubleday Dell. A freelance writer and editor since 1996, Stephanie, who holds a B.A. in English literature from Amherst College, now specializes in non-fiction books primarily in the areas of self-help, health, spirituality, and new thought. Books on complementary and alternative medicine are a subspecialty she particularly enjoys because she is a fourth-level Reiki master teacher and has benefitted so much personally from receiving acupuncture, massage therapy, and chiropractic treatment.

To write Stephanie or inquire about her writing services, speaking programs, or online courses, please contact her through her website: StephanieGunning.com.

"The three C's of life: choices, chances, and changes. You must make a choice to take a chance or your life will never change."
—JoJo

Dare to live your life full out!

www.ingramcontent.com/pod-product-compliance
Lightning Source LLC
Chambersburg PA
CBHW021930190326
41519CB00009B/973